Desert Sorrow

Tom Mann spent his early days in Elgin, Morayshire, Scotland, and migrated to Australia in 1964 after graduating in Science at Aberdeen University. His agricultural and teaching career included two years as a high school teacher and twenty years as a lecturer at the Roseworthy Campus (formerly Roseworthy Agricultural College) of the University of Adelaide. He also worked with the Department of Agriculture, the CSIRO Division of Nutrition and Biochemistry in South Australia and on agricultural projects as a consultant in Algeria, Pakistan, India, Bangladesh and China. After leaving Roseworthy in 1994, Tom completed a PhD on a rural development study in West Timor, as well as a certificate for teaching English to speakers of other languages. He commenced as an education officer with the Woomera detention centre in October 2000. From his personal experiences he wrote this account to help promote a better understanding of asylum seekers. Tom and his wife, Liz, live in Gawler, close to the vineyards of the Barossa Valley in South Australia, and have two daughters, Rachel and Linda.

Desert Sorrow

Asylum seekers at Woomera

Tom Mann

Wakefield
Press

Wakefield Press
1 The Parade West
Kent Town
South Australia 5067
www.wakefieldpress.com.au

First published by Seaview Press 2003
Wakefield Press edition published 2003

Typeset by Clinton Ellicott, Wakefield Press
Printed by Hyde Park Press, Adelaide

National Library of Australia
Cataloguing-in-publication entry

Mann, Tom, 1941– .
Desert sorrow: asylum seekers at Woomera.

Bibliography.
ISBN 1 86254 623 1.

1. Woomera Immigration Reception and Processing Centre. 2. Alien detention
centers—South Australia—Woomera. 3. Refugees—South Australia—
Woomera. 4. Illegal aliens—South Australia —Woomera. I. Title.

325.210994

Contents

Foreword   vi

Acknowledgements   viii

Author's Note   ix

INTRODUCTION   1

BEHIND THE RAZOR WIRE   5

TIME OUT FROM WOOMERA   31

WOOMERA UNFOLDS   37

OVERLOAD AT WOOMERA   85

A FLAWED PROCESS AND LENGTHY DELAYS   132

A BETTER WAY?   151

BEHIND AND BEYOND THE WIRE   159

WOOMERA CLOSES   194

Glossary and Abbreviations   198

Bibliography   205

Foreword

Australia has in recent years implemented harsh measures on refugees and asylum seekers, changing laws, retrospectively where necessary, to make anti-asylum seeker policy legal. These measures have been as popular as they have been misrepresented and misunderstood.

The system is designed to intimidate and torment and so to provide a deterrent to other refugees fleeing persecution and seeking a country that is a signatory to the 1951 Convention. It is also designed, through fiddling with legislation, to restrict the number of people, regardless of the refugee status, eligible for protection in Australia under our international convention obligations.

Central to the success of the mandatory detention policy is the invisibility of those detained. Australians have rarely received a true picture of the men women and children imprisoned, in many cases indefinitely, in the detention centres. Invisible and silenced, these people have been demonised first as queue jumpers, then, as their desperation increases, as criminals and undesirables. The only time media access to the detention centres is unrestricted and encouraged is when there is something negative, and dehumanising, to report.

Mandatory detention has been a resounding success story for the current government but at an as yet poorly estimated human cost. Tom Mann's book gives us the beginnings of an understanding of the effects of this policy, both in terms of the uncertainty and anguish suffered by families and particularly children in detention, and in terms of our own culpability in having let this happen in Australia.

Tom Mann is a well-educated, well-travelled Australian, someone who has enough experiences of other cultures to cut through the prejudices and fears that blind many Australians to Middle Eastern cultures. He has worked in Indonesia, Pakistan, Bangladesh, Algeria and China. His quiet, matter-of-fact prose records with little commentary what he saw and experienced as a teacher and as Education Officer in Woomera IRPC (Immigration Reception and Processing Centre), taking the reader in and leaving us to think through what we have experienced with him.

Through reading this book I got a deeper sense of how critical a punishment deprivation of freedom is, and how terrible to impose this deprivation on people without trial, without crime, and without any certain release date. I have also kept with me a sense of the messiness of policy in action and a strong sense of the culture of punishment and disempowerment that pervades and wears people down over the months and years. And I got a sense of children in detention, not as a kind of collective pawn for government or for activist groups, but as individuals both resilient and hurt, children we have damaged and go on damaging.

The great achievement of this book is that the people Tom Mann introduces to the reader are real, not figments of media construction, and we get to care about them, and worry for them.

Eva Sallis

It is really an awesome gift from God that someone is offered the opportunity of knowing one's own reality. This opportunity may be compulsory or mandatory like, for example, detention for an indefinite period in a bad place. Detention which has been deliberately set to be punitive, daunting and enigmatic for a group of people called 'refugees' or 'asylum seekers', and whose bad luck and cursed souls lead them to face indisputable and mandatory sufferings. I'm one of them. Yet, the reader may conclude from these words that detention may be useful for some people with special regard to one's self-recognition, but I tell you: 'Yes, it could be, but for quite a limited time, because if it was prolonged for an indefinite time and without any logical reason, then the most important consequences will be sorrow, wrath, frustration and pain.'

Dr Amir Al-Obaidi

Acknowledgements

I am indebted to editorial comments and suggestions from Jan McInerney, Pat Sheahan, Dr Amir Al-Obaidi, Eva Sallis, Bill Phippard of Seaview Press, and Kevin Liston. For their artwork, I thank Chris Crothers, Sadiq for permission to use his drawings, including the one used on the back cover, Alamdar for permission to use his sketches, Jeremy Moore for provision of children's artwork, Helena Turinski for her graphic design of the book cover, and Peter Mathew for permission to use his photos of the detention centre, including the one used for the front cover.

I would also like to express my appreciation to the following for their encouragement: Sonia Wilson, Inese Petersen, Pam Jones, Garry Bickley, Ray Hartigan, Hafez Zamani, Mary Retallack, Megan Philpott, Kevin and Liz Munro, Susan Stevens, Jan Miller, Max Randall, and to my daughters, Rachel and Linda. Many others provided useful comments.

I especially owe a debt of gratitude to my wife, Liz, who supported me in so many ways while at Woomera and during the writing of this book.

Author's Note

There are many stories to tell from those who have lived in a detention centre for asylum seekers and from those who have worked in one. This is just one of them. For those on the outside looking in, the truth is elusive—shackled in by the constraints of a security system not amenable to free access by individuals, the media and concerned groups of people. Despite this, a story emerges which causes us to reflect on the kind of response to those who are not so fortunate as us. This book attempts to open a few more pages of that story. In the end, I hope that truth will triumph.

The first names of the asylum seekers have been used and these have been changed where details about them have been given, except where agreement has been obtained or where their names have already been publicised through the media. Only first names are used for the employees at the Woomera detention centre and for others except where they are well known in the public arena.

The acronym DIMA (Department of Immigration and Multicultural Affairs) was changed to DIMIA (Department of Immigration, Multicultural and Indigenous Affairs) in the latter part of 2001. For ease of reading the current acronym DIMIA is used throughout the book.

INTRODUCTION

Successive governments of Australia have maintained a mandatory detention policy with bipartisan support since its introduction in 1992.

The purpose of mandatory detention is to ensure that unauthorised arrivals are readily available while their identity is established, and to facilitate health, character and security assessments. It enables the processing of their claims for refugee status and their availability for removal if they have no lawful basis for remaining in Australia.

Underpinning the policy of mandatory detention is Australia's *Migration Act 1958* that requires all non-Australians who are unlawfully in mainland Australia to be detained and that unless they are granted permission to remain in Australia they must be removed as soon as possible.

The Woomera Immigration and Reception and Processing Centre (Woomera IPRC) opened on 28 November 1999. Woomera is 480 kilometres north west of Adelaide. The first intake of 358 detainees was on 30 November 1999. By 24 February 2000 the number of detainees had risen to 1290.

Australasian Correctional Management (ACM), a subsidiary of an American firm, Wackenhurt, managed the six Australian detention centres—at Port Hedland, Curtin and Perth in Western Australia, Woomera on Commonwealth land in South Australia, Maribyrnong in Melbourne and Villawood in Sydney.

The overall responsibility for the care of detainees at the detention centres belonged to the Department of Immigration,

Multicultural and Indigenous Affairs (DIMIA). DIMIA staff decided whether or not the detainees were to receive a three-year temporary visa. Australia, by law, required all asylum seekers who arrived without valid visas to be detained until their status is determined.

Most detainees were from Afghanistan, Iraq and Iran. There were also smaller numbers from Morocco, Algeria, Palestine and elsewhere. Some adult detainees arrived with, or without, their families, others were single adults, and there were also a number of unaccompanied children. After a sea voyage from Indonesia the asylum seekers landed at Ashmore Reef or Christmas Island, having undertaken a journey from their homeland with the help of people smugglers. DIMIA officials then organised their ongoing flight to one of the detention centres—usually Woomera, Curtin or Port Hedland.

On 8 June 2000 about 500 detainees broke out of the Woomera detention centre and walked three kilometres to the Woomera town square, where they staged a peaceful demonstration before returning to the detention centre. They had wanted to protest against living conditions and delays in processing their applications.

On 13 June 2000 the Minister for Immigration, Philip Ruddock, addressed the delegates of the detainees. He told them that they had come to Australia illegally and without documents in most cases. This had caused delays in processing. The asylum seekers had to be kept in detention while their claims were being processed. They should have done the right thing and contacted the United Nations High Commissioner for Refugees (UNHCR) or any of the Australian embassies. Mr Ruddock continued to emphasise there would be no shortcuts. There was a responsibility to consider the health, safety and security of the Australian community. In assessing applications, officers had to find out about their identities, where they had lived, and to know that they had not been criminals.

Soon after the minister's visit, the first of the asylum seekers were released with their temporary protection visas. There was frustration for those who remained and about 100 detainees faced deportation after having their claims for refugee status rejected. On 28 August 2000, 80 detainees rioted, burning the school and five other buildings.

About this time I applied for a position as an education officer with Australasian Correctional Management (ACM). After an interview and police clearance ACM gave me the green light to start on 30 September. The first six-week contract was followed by a six-month one from 5 March 2001.

I have attempted to describe my personal experiences with asylum seekers during and after my employment at the Woomera detention centre. I have also tried to describe the personal stories of detainees and give a perspective of what it was like inside the centre. Issues relating to the asylum seekers emerge as the Woomera story unfolds. Hopefully, this will lead to a better understanding of asylum seekers as well as provide some snapshots of detention life

Map showing detention centres in Australia

BEHIND THE RAZOR WIRE
(1 October–12 November 2000)

The flight from Adelaide to the modern township of Roxby Downs took about an hour—time enough to wonder what I would be doing for the next six weeks, away from my wife and two grown-up daughters. I had responded to an article in *The Advertiser* about a need for an education officer. With images of demonstrators and the August riots still fresh in my memory, I wondered what I had let myself in for.

From the air, Roxby Downs seemed like an attractive oasis set in a reddish-brown landscape of scattered shrubs and small trees. Nearby, Olympic Dam prospered with its mining of high quality copper, uranium, gold and silver.

The security officer from the Woomera detention centre, who had been assigned to pick me up, had fallen asleep. After I had waited for about 20 minutes, looking at the mining display boards outside the air terminal, Alan appeared and apologised for his catnap.

We stopped at the modern shopping complex in Roxby Downs. The town offered a comprehensive range of commercial, educational and sporting facilities to more than 4000 residents, many of whom were working at the mining site of Olympic Dam Corporation.

Then we travelled for 50 minutes along a sealed road to Woomera, passing sand dunes covered with mulga, native pines and hopbush, and intervening tracts of mostly saltbush, bluebush and western myall. As we neared Woomera, larger areas of gibber plains dominated the scene with smaller shrub species.

The water tanks, a prominent feature of Woomera, came into view, as well as the fenced perimeter of the Woomera Immigration, Reception and Processing Centre (WIRPC)—just three kilometres outside the town.

Alan left me at one of 12 units in a two-storeyed accommodation block. I had the rest of the weekend to fill in before fronting up at the detention centre. I set out to explore the Woomera town, known to the locals as 'an oasis in the desert'.

An apt name for the town, 'woomera' was used by the Australian Aborigines to describe a type of throwing stick for propelling a spear. From spears to rockets, Woomera in the South Australian outback was established in 1947 as a joint project with the United Kingdom for testing experimental rockets and missiles. Later the European Launcher Development Organisation (ELDO) designed and built the Europa series of rockets. Names such as *Jindivik*, an Australian designed and built pilotless target aircraft, and *Thunderbird*, a ground-to-air, anti-aircraft missile, appeared. The *Black Arrow* was a three-stage British rocket used to place two satellites into orbit from Woomera. The United States of America also operated a deep tracking station at Island Lagoon, about 25 kilometres south of Woomera.

Len Beadell, who has been called the last of the true Australian explorers, carried out the initial surveys needed to establish the Woomera Rocket Range. Len was also the author of six best-selling books about his experiences in the outback of Australia. The Woomera Prohibited Area for testing rockets and long-range weapons stretched towards Western Australia and is still the largest land-locked area in the world, covering an area of 127,000 km.

Dr William Alan Butement came to Australia in 1946 to assist in establishing the Woomera Rocket Range. He inspired the development of the *Malkara* anti-tank weapon, the *Ikara* anti-submarine weapon, over-the-horizon radar and the *Barra* sonobuoy system—a sonar device used to detect submerged submarines.

In its heyday Woomera boasted a population of more than 6000.

In 2000, with some 350 residents, the town basked in its once secret past, provided services for the detention centre as well as passing travellers, and looked forward to a new phase of aerospace development. Kistler Aerospace, an American company, was expected to build a launch facility in Woomera for the world's first reusable launch vehicle for low earth satellites. A Japanese project, expected to be under way in 2002, aimed to provide research and development for the next generation of supersonic passenger aircraft.

In the centre of town I visited a missile park, displaying different types of rockets, aircraft and weapons. And nearby I spent two hours at the Heritage Centre, absorbed in the displays and accounts of the various rocket and satellite programs. A supermarket and variety store provided most household items. There were ample recreational facilities—a tribute to the American presence, I suspected. They included a picture theatre, fitness centre, modern swimming pool, squash courts, tennis courts, bowling greens, a tenpin bowling alley, golf course, a sports oval, and, of course, there were gaming machines and pool tables at the Eldo Hotel.

The Eldo Hotel and a caravan park provided most of the accommodation facilities. Originally established in the 1960s for housing the personnel involved in the space program, the Eldo had 200 air-conditioned rooms, a fully licensed restaurant, a bar and a large function room. The caravan park, named the Woomera Travellers Village, provided rooms for backpackers and powered sites for caravans. After spending half a day and maybe a night at Woomera, travellers could follow the Stuart Highway to explore the opal mining dugouts of Coober Pedy or northwards to Roxby Downs and Andamooka, another opal-mining town.

A five-kilometre jogging track skirted the town with low-lying scrub and a water pipeline from Port Augusta on the southern side. To the north was Breen Park, designed for family relaxation with tall, shady eucalypts, lush lawns, a bird sanctuary—mostly housing

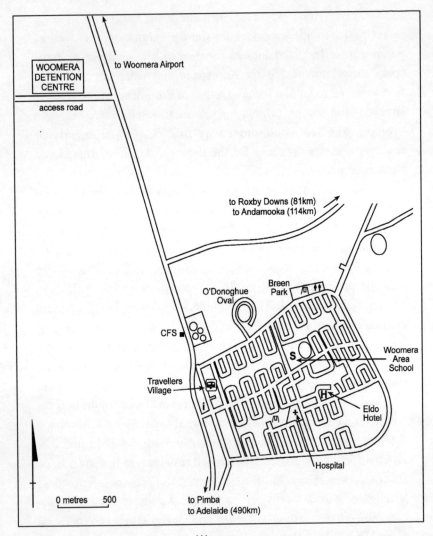

Woomera

different species of parrots—and electric barbecues. Not far from Breen Park was O'Donoghue Oval and nearby Woomera Sports Club—another popular 'watering hole'. A little further towards the Roxby Downs road was the cemetery. Many of those buried were infants and middle-aged men. Later, I asked some current and past residents about this but there was no clear explanation apart from deaths due to road accidents and disease.

At night-time the floodlights of the detention centre lit up the sky as though a small city had come to life.

The Heritage Centre had also provided me with information on the Woomera IRPC, which was commonly known as the Woomera detention centre. According to the federal Department of Immigration, Multicultural and Indigenous Affairs (DIMIA) the 'boat people' detained there have come to Australia unlawfully. They are asylum seekers who seek protection as refugees under the 1951 United Nations Convention Relating to the Status of Refugees and 1967 Protocol Relating to the Status of Refugees. The Convention defines refugees as people outside their country of nationality or their usual country of residence who are unable or unwilling to return or to seek the protection of that country, due to a well-founded fear of being persecuted for reasons of race, religion, nationality, membership of a particular social group or political opinion.

When I first arrived at the Woomera detention centre on 1 October 2000 the perimeter fencing topped by razor wire unnerved me with its prison-like appearance. I passed through the main checkpoint as a busload of detainees was about to leave for Adelaide. Inside was an assortment of semi-permanent and trans portable buildings forming the administrative and services complex. The complex offended any reasonable sense of artistic beauty.

Internal fencing separated the administration and services area from the compounds in which the detainees were housed. I observed some detainees walking slowly across the dusty, gravelly area while others swept the concrete surrounds of the administrative area. A few isolated trees and a row of shrubs nearby offered little consolation to the stark layout.

Trish, the programs manager, introduced me to all her staff — Mary, Frossine, Jamal and Mehrdad, the interpreters; Christine

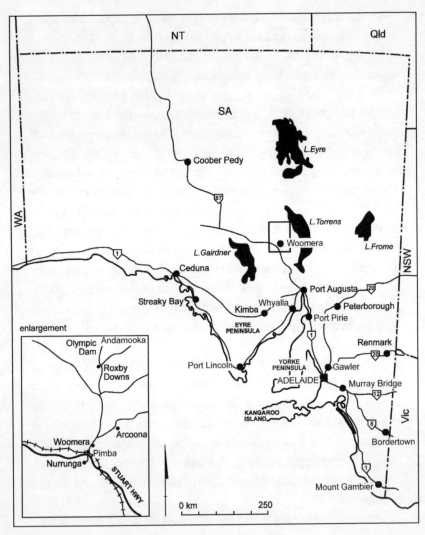

South Australia

and Margota, the education officers; Harold, the psychologist; Alley and Kylie, the welfare officers; John and Jennifer, the recreation officers; and Rosetta and Janine, the counsellors.

The programs officers were responsible for social welfare, education, recreation and interpreting services. In all, 53 types of programs were listed to cater for the detainees. They included various sports, art, music, craft, fitness, sewing, mural painting and teaching activities. An Australian State police officer talked about civil issues such as the law and motor vehicle registration. Then there could be specific programs for men, women and children, such as a women's alternative therapy group, unaccompanied minors' activities, a children's after-school club and a kindergarten.

The high risk assessment team (HRAT), which included a social welfare officer and a psychologist, met twice a week to facilitate assessment and care of detainees who were at risk of self-harm or suicide. The programs officers assisted in this area by providing suitable activities and therapeutic sessions.

On 27 September, just before I started with Australasian Correctional Management (ACM), Trish, the programs manager, had met with the managing director of ACM, Kevin Lewis, the vice chairman of the board of Wackenhut Corrections Corporation, George Foley, and centre manager of Woomera IRPC, Jim Meakins, to discuss the current and future programs for detainees.

From a survey carried out by the programs staff, Trish had pointed out to the managers that detainees were fearful of not getting a visa, of never seeing their families again, of being sent back to their country, of being 'lost' in the DIMIA/ACM system, of being locked up and of not getting help from a doctor if needed. The highest priority of the detainees was to obtain a visa. In the high-priority category there was a need to have more frequent access to DIMIA concerning their cases, access to telephones, a high standard of education for their children, privacy and dignity and the opportunity to see a doctor more freely than a nurse. Important, but not so high on the priority list, was access to television and radios, job opportunities, to be able to cook or at least be supplied with more culturally appropriate food, to make or buy their own clothes, to have hygienic and pleasant surroundings, to have hot water and homely facilities, and to have respect and understanding from officers and staff. Trish then discussed the implications of these findings for the adoption of suitable programs that would have a positive influence on the lives of detainees.

Australasian Correctional Management was a private company—a subsidiary of Wackenhut Corrections Corporation (WCC), a United States company that bore the name of its founder and owner, George Wackenhut. ACM managed the detention facilities, provided services to the detainees and met duty-of-care obligations. DIMIA had overall responsibility for the allocation of resources as well as the design, establishment and management of the centre and the care of the detainees. For the first year, most of the ACM security staff were on six-week detachments from other ACM-managed correctional and detention centres in Australia and New Zealand.

Christine and Margota showed me the educational facilities in the main compound—all fairly new as everything had been burnt down in the recent riot. Christine had done a mammoth job in starting all over again. With three classrooms and a library we were in business. Each classroom was 12 metres long by three and a half metres wide—totally unsuitable for teaching, as we would find out later. After the tour the three of us discussed how we might run the classes. Teaching would start the next day.

As teachers, we would be completely responsible for the educational needs of children and adults. Apart from the provisions of basic teaching facilities and financial assistance for the purchase of teaching aids and materials, we would not receive any assistance from ACM, DIMIA, of Federal or State education departments with regard to the kind of educational program. For the children, the teaching curriculum would be ad hoc and we would devise a syllabus for each subject. As we had only three classrooms there would be little opportunity to separate them according to age, gender, ability or country background.

After one day at the Woomera detention centre I realised I had crossed the divide to a completely different world, a world that was

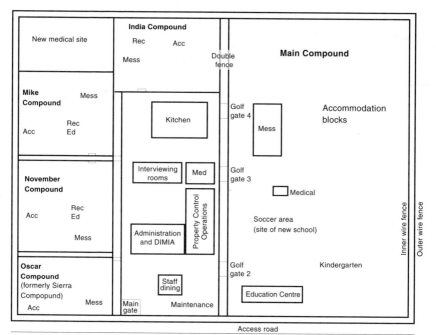

Rec = Recreation centre   Ed = Education centre   Acc = Accommodation units   Med = Medical

Woomera Detention Centre (August 2001)

about to unfold, more than I would realise, to expose the characters and plights of people fleeing from their home countries. The world inside the centre would also expose us as Australians—our weaknesses and strengths, our compassion and contempt, our attitudes, beliefs and fears.

The next day I was about to start my teaching duties when Trish gave me a 20-minute orientation on what to do and say in all kinds of situations. Words such as 'visa', 'lawyer', and 'refugees' were best not used. The 'detainees' were really 'residents'. Also the 'residents' were being 'inducted', not 'imprisoned'.

Radio contact was necessary at all times. If there were a dangerous situation I was to leave at once. If someone was wounded or sick I should report the incident after giving immediate aid. Be careful with blood though—use gloves from my first-aid pouch.

Watch your tongue. Be on guard at all times—the residents would be up to every trick imaginable and more. Write referral notes and record all untoward activities. There were a number of 'nevers'. Never allow yourself to become involved with immigration issues or to approach DIMIA without the consent of the centre manager. Never bring in or take out an unauthorised item without the permission of the centre manager. Never accept or give a gift of any kind. Never show favouritism.

On a display board at the back of our office area I gazed at a curious display of objects seized from Woomera detainees. They included doorknob knives, a range of piercing and cutting instruments, a spiked knuckleduster, a pair of pliers, half a garden shear, a razor-headed toothbrush and two nooses.

With some apprehension, I was released into the compound for my first contact with the young ones. We walked about 120 metres from the entrance of the main compound, called Golf Three gate, to the education centre of three classrooms and a library. Not far from the education complex was a liaison post where detainees were assembling to make requests for their daily needs, such as soap, toothpaste and washing powder.

The young children were rowdy but keen on colouring and drawing. Then I had a session with the intermediates, followed by an older group for mathematics. I tried to stay afloat and soon realised that teaching children with little understanding of the English language was going to be quite a challenge. In the afternoon I taught about kangaroos and wombats and read an illustrated children's storybook.

The next day was visa day. Every Tuesday and Thursday expectations rose. Twenty-one detainees left but the mood of the centre was low with some having been there for more than 10 months. Often there was only an hour's notice for those released and hardly any opportunity for celebration or saying goodbye. In case they were being released that day children often stayed with their parents and did not attend school in the morning. Most of the children

The Main Compound showing accommodation blocks.

turned up in the afternoon and Margota organised them for reading, drawing and games. Three adult detainees assisted us with reading exercises.

That evening, in my unit, I felt like a rookie as I watched an SBS television documentary examining the treatment of detainees at Woomera. Mary Lindsay, a migration agent, decried the pitiful conditions and the poor support services once they had been released into the community. Others supported her in attacking the Government's overall approach to asylum seekers. One of the comments made about the Woomera centre was that there was 'no playground, no grass and no school'. Strictly speaking there was no school building but there were classes for children in improvised demountables or 'dongas', as they were commonly known. It was also claimed that there were 'no rights to family reunion and social services', as granted to refugees coming to Australia through the appropriate channels.

Every day we would pass through the Golf Three gate into the main compound. A security officer would unlock the gate; another sitting at a desk would then record our call number—education

A Woomera welcome showing outer palisade fence topped by
razor wire and inner perimeter fence.

three in my case—and the time we entered. If we were carrying our
radios and not bringing in contraband we would be allowed
through. Often detainees would mill around the gate waiting to pass
through to the administrative and services complex for medical
treatment, work duties, phoning or making contact with the interpreters and DIMIA.

A small medical centre was set up in a donga near the gate. Here
the Australian Red Cross often assisted people by providing tracing
and messaging services to enable detainees to re-establish and
maintain contact with their family as well as providing humanitarian assistance when required.

During the next few days, I started to get into the swing of
teaching mathematics and English to the young children, aged
from five to seven. They were rather restless but when they settled
down to their exercises they seemed happy. Any colouring com-
bined with the elementary mathematics was always a plus. One
who appeared a little more restless than most was a bright young
lad, Shayan. His parents said they had fled political persecution in

The desolate landscape surrounding the Woomera town and
detention centre.

Iran. With a bit of coaxing and extra attention Shayan responded
and joined in with the activities. I had no idea at the time of the
trauma and suffering that would befall him.

The older children were very lively and needed to be chal-
lenged as well as entertained. The art and craft activities absorbed
their interest. Our enlisted assistant detainee teachers explained in
Farsi and Arabic what we would do and this helped a great deal;
otherwise, if we had a class on our own most of the exercises had
to be almost self-explanatory.

On Friday, 7 October 2000, a meeting was held in the mess of
the main compound. The head of DIMIA at Woomera, Tony
Hamilton-Smith, addressed the detainees concerning the delays in
processing of claims. Well over 200 men and women packed the
mess to hear the latest on the outcome of progress in their cases.
I stood at the front along with the interpreters and other officers.
Looking out over a sea of mostly brown, non-European, faces I
felt, for a moment, I was in a foreign country. There was a sense
of uneasiness as the detainees listened attentively to the Farsi
and Arabic versions of Tony's explanation of the delays in the
processing of cases. According to Tony, the case officers had

processed 95 per cent of cases for a primary decision on their refugee application. Some would have to go through further processing, though, with appeals to the Refugee Review Tribunal and to the Federal Court.

After Tony's address, hands shot up in the air. A barrage of questions followed and even a youngster and a mother attempted to have their say above the interjections. The mood became more intense and some became quite agitated. At this point, Tony allowed four more questions. One of the men said that Iraqis from Syria were being discriminated against and waved a letter to support his case. After the meeting, anyone who seemed approachable, especially the interpreters, was a target for further queries. Agitation among the men increased and the security officers rushed in but gradually everything simmered down. Many questions, though, weren't answered.

At the close of Friday I was beginning to come to terms with my new environment. It was a landmark but the first week was not over yet. Saturday was orientation day. After all our training sessions of what to do and what not to do in different circumstances we went through firefighting drills, donned riot gear and were taught how to use a baton and a gas gun. How could an ex-Roseworthy agricultural lecturer end up in a job like this?

Later we walked through the compounds to see for ourselves the evidence of the recent riots in August: scorched earth and stones, the removal of concrete facing from the barrack-type buildings which had been used as missiles, and places where the fencing had been broken through using iron bars. According to reports, there had been a peaceful protest the previous day but during the night security officers had gone into the dongas to round up ringleaders to take them to a compound named Sierra. One of the women must have thought she was back in her home country and had begun screaming and tearing her clothes. The whole compound had erupted and gone on a rampage. The school had been among six buildings destroyed.

That evening I had dinner at the Eldo Hotel with John, an activities officer, and afterwards we played pool. John was from Sudan and could easily identify with some of the problems faced by the detainees, as he had spent several months in a Rwandan refugee camp. He spoke Arabic and mixed freely as he tried to facilitate sporting activities—mainly table tennis, volleyball and football.

The following Monday it was a full house for teaching. I tackled writing numbers with the 5–7-year-olds, Australian money with the 8–11s and reading with the 12–17s. There was a session given over to board and card games such as chess, Uno, and snakes-and-ladders. Then in the afternoon there were classes for tae-kwondo and dancing. The detainee assistant teachers helped a lot. Reading the illustrated children's stories proved to be a favourite. On one occasion I was reading a story when a fly entered my mouth. The children looked aghast at my paroxysmal outburst—the story had definitely taken on a new twist.

At the Eldo Hotel that evening everyone shared experiences. The social welfare people had had a bad day with one woman threatening to kill herself if she were not released the next day. John experienced difficulties with running sporting activities because of restrictions imposed by the security staff. Frossine, the Arabic interpreter, talked about some distressing situations for the detainees with regard to their processing by DIMIA.

It became a common event with 10 or more of us walking up to the Eldo each night for dinner and freely unloading. The fact that eavesdroppers could pick up choice pieces of conversation for further release did not seem to bother us. After the informal debriefing session, we would adjourn to the saloon bar for some games of pool.

The next day 16 detainees were released, happy and relieved to know their temporary protection visas (TPVs) had been granted. The woman who had threatened to kill herself was among them and everyone breathed a little easier. For those who had been there more than nine months there was still a vestige of hope. But the forlorn looks on their faces told of their own personal suffering. According to the psychologists, many were depressed and some suicidal.

DIMIA had arranged three interviews for an applicant claiming refugee status. The first interview was carried out within days of arrival by the border control and compliance section of DIMIA to identify the person and gather intelligence relating to the route taken to reach Australia and assistance given by smugglers; and also to determine whether the person had a prima facie story which engaged Australia's protection obligations. If there was not sufficient evidence to engage that obligation the applicant was screened out and could go no further in making a claim.

As well as security and intelligence debriefings a medical check was carried out. New arrivals were separated from other detainees in the centre. The DIMIA business manager at Woomera coordinated the department's process of examining applications for protection.

At the second interview a migration agent assisted the applicant make a claim. The Immigration Asylum Advice and Assistance Scheme (IAAAS), funded by the Australian Government, provided the migration agent as a legal representative to the applicant. At the third or protection application interview, a case officer of DIMIA, acting as a delegate of the minister, made a primary decision on the application for a temporary protection visa. This interview, according to DIMIA, was with a highly trained immigration officer. The case officer assessed the claim against UN criteria set out in the 1951 Convention, the 1967 Protocol on the Status of Refugees, and Country Information Systems.

Where an application was refused, a person could seek a merits review of that decision from an independent tribunal—either the Refugee Review Tribunal (RRT) or the Administrative Appeals Tribunal (AAT), depending on the basis for refusal. If a person were refused at the RRT stage there was still a chance, much smaller chance, of a favourable decision at the Federal Court, for judicial review on the grounds of error of law. If an appeal to the Federal Court was successful the case was reviewed once more by the RRT. It could take seven to eight months for an application before a single Federal Court judge and a further four to five months for an appeal to the Full Federal Court. Then the applicant could even appeal to the High Court for the matter to be heard there and finally to the Minister of Immigration. To exhaust all the legal avenues could take a number of years, during which the law required the applicant to remain in detention.

On the teaching side, we decided to have an art exhibition. Margota organised some of the children to cut out foam shapes and stick them on to cardboard plates. Some of the girls strung lines of colourful beads together while the boys made Indian headbands, complete with coloured feathers. Others painted Australian animals, cut them out and made a collage on butcher's paper. In the afternoon, painting activities followed the reading session. One lad excelled at drawing helicopters and rockets. It was a pity we couldn't take him to Woomera to view some of the rockets on display.

On another occasion we captured the creative talents of the children with a dinosaur theme. They had a great time drawing, painting and making models of clay dinosaurs. As it was so successful we ran the project for several days.

Later, Christine, who had been at the Woomera centre for over four months, described the state of men and women in the compound named India as desperate. Some of the women had sewn their lips together as a form of protest; they had become so withdrawn and depressed about their future. And many would be separated from their families for at least three years if they obtained a temporary visa—something they could not have foreseen.

We decided to test the waters for adult teaching of English and life skills. After spreading the word, 27 people crowded into one of the small teaching rooms. I spoke about the importance of learning English for living in Australia before answering questions on employment prospects, finding jobs and buying a car. We arranged to meet again to start English classes.

Harold, the psychologist, organised a bus to go to Roxby for dinner. So that night all the programs staff let off steam recounting Woomera events at the Chinese restaurant there.

An example: one detainee had collapsed on the ground. A security officer asked the detainees, 'Is there anyone here who speaks English?'

'Yes, I do,' another officer had piped up.

The following day Harold let us know he had eight people on the HRAT (High Risk Assessment Team) plan. A person assessed as a 'high risk' had to be carefully monitored with a program to bring the person back to a stable state. One Afghani person had swallowed more than a kilogram of small rocks and had had to be rushed to the hospital for surgery.

English teaching to the adult men in the main compound started in earnest the following week, with about 20 turning up after the last children's class in the afternoon. They responded well and seemed keen to learn. There was a wide range of abilities and I could see we should really split the class into two: one for beginners and one for the more advanced. We were limited, though, because of the priority given to children's classes.

In the third week I finally made my way over to India compound, where most of the Afghani people were housed. Most of them had been in for more than nine months and were quite despondent. I met Alif and Abdullah, both good English speakers. We talked for about half an hour. Others joined and all were keen to air their grievances. One person said, 'Even if I get released, I do not want to stay in Australia after what they have done to us.'

Another said, 'The troublemakers have been released but not us. Why? Even after three months sometimes they are released. It's not fair. There's no information given to us. No news. No progress report. Why do they keep us here for so long?'

'If we go through the proper channels we have to wait 76 weeks in Pakistan. It's not possible. In Pakistan it's almost as bad as in Afghanistan,' someone else commented.

And so the complaints went on. One of the main problems was that the detainees were cut off from the outside world. There was no television, radio or newspapers. We arranged some times for English classes though I wondered about the response given their despondent state.

At the weekly programs staff meeting, comments were made on the brusqueness of some of the officers. Trish commented that some of the officers did have a 'correctional attitude'.

One of the young lads, Ahmed, a 12-year-old, preferred to do light duties, such as sweeping, rather than come to classes. Christine and I began to encourage him to come to school. At first he refused; then he said he might come. And a few days later he turned up so we made a special fuss of him and I took him aside for reading practice. He took to the reading with gusto and soon we were reading all the adventure books we could find. His reading and English comprehension improved dramatically. He was always willing to help in any classroom duties, such as cleaning the classroom. I would greet Ahmed's father daily while he tended the grassy patch outside the administration block. Ahmed was a bright lad and continued to come to school regularly until a further complication set in. He and his father received undue press coverage two months later over an allegation of child abuse that had not been fully examined at the time. According to the centre manager, it had not merited further investigation.

The days started to fill up with teaching children from 9 am to 3 pm, followed by adult English classes for men. Margota and Christine taught the women. Initially the response in India compound was good with about 12 Afghani men turning up. It was very informal. They found out I had been in the North-West Frontier Province of Pakistan for a year and that I knew some Pushto. When I asked for *tor chai* (black tea) they were very happy to oblige.

I brought in some newspapers and we looked at the employment advertisements and talked about how we might find a job. After a week I could sense that they were becoming more depressed with the apparent hopelessness of their cases. Some of them preferred to withdraw into themselves and even sleep the day away.

As the Afghanis had been separated from the others, the English teaching was mostly to the Iraqis and Iranians in the main compound. It was more organised and we settled into a routine of conversational practice sessions interspersed with information on Australia and life skills. The lessons seemed to go well, with lots of participation. Many of them could speak a faltering style of English so I pitched the material at their level. Unfortunately, I could see some of those who could hardly speak at all were becoming rather restless so I tried to include them in conversational practice.

One of the Iranians in the main compound came to me and asked if he could write his personal story so that I could correct it. Alex wrote that he was of Kurdish background born in 1974 and from an aristocratic family. The family was very religious but he himself was not and did not know why. As a 17-year-old schoolboy he had been arrested by the intelligence service while giving a speech at an unofficial meeting. He had been kept in a cell for the next 34 days and this had given him an opportunity to think a lot about his beliefs.

On being released, Alex had studied philosophy and read the works of writers such as Plato, Aristotle, Thomas Aquinas, Machiavelli, Hegel and Marx. As well, he read widely on works of writers such as Lukacs Gyorgy and Mikhail Sholokhov, who had influenced the mainstream of communist thought in the first half of the 20th century. He had become a communist, but 'a new one with new thoughts'. Alex commenced studying medicine because the social conditions in Iran oppressed him. And medical students were respected. He had continued as an activist, becoming the secretary of the Students' United Front in his province, secretary of a Kurdish students' organisation and editor of a students' weekly newspaper. He had played an important part in the student demonstration of

India Compound

Photograph obtained from the Human Rights and Equal Opportunity
Commission's National Inquiry into Children in Immigration Detention:
reproduced from website http://www.humanrights.gov.au/index.html

July 1999. Following the demonstration he had been arrested and
sentenced to five years' imprisonment. Somehow he had managed
to escape and found his way to Australia.

There were a number of highly qualified people in the centre. One
of these was Dr Amir, a 49-year-old Iraqi, who had earned an
international reputation as a microbiologist. He had studied at
Baghdad's College of Veterinary Medicine before accepting a
scholarship to Bristol University for research in veterinary public
health. He gained his PhD for research work on campylobacter, a
bacteria carrying infections from animals to humans. Dr Amir
returned to Baghdad but his appointment to a select team of scien-
tists by Saddam Hussein for a new academy of microbiology and
genetic engineering compromised his values concerning human
life. He decided to leave Iraq via the smuggling route, leaving
behind his wife and two children.

Dr Amir would spend 11 months in the centre. About six
months before I arrived Dr Amir organised a teaching program for

detainees, aged 16–20. He took classes in English and biology while others taught physics and mathematics. The interest was strong at first but tailed off when some of the students began to regret coming to Australia since there was little progress in their cases. Some preferred to work to earn money while others lost interest in studying.

As a specialist in bacteriology and bacterial food-borne illnesses, Dr Amir confirmed that during his time in the detention centre he had seen many problems with various infections. Children who had no recreational facilities would play on the coarse pebbly soil, he said. Wounds would become infected with purulent discharges and sometimes affect the pelvic lymph nodes. After long waiting periods, they would be put on a course of antibiotic treatment. Also, many detainees would show varying symptoms of gastrointestinal disturbances with mild to severe abdominal pain, nausea and vomiting, and diarrhoea ranging from mild watery stools to severe bloody or mucoid types. Dr Amir attributed some of these problems to food-borne illnesses. As some people lacked a basic understanding of health matters, they had usually neglected medical check-ups or discontinued treatment. Another problem had been the outbreak of typhoid fever he attributed to poor toilet hygiene and the general lack of hygiene measures to prevent an infected person spreading the disease. He had often made written suggestions to the medical centre regarding the risks but had received no reply.

Dr Amir described some of his impressions of those early days at Woomera:

At the beginning of April 2000 there were more than 1400 detainees, most coming from either Iraq or Iran or Afghanistan as well as some from Palestine, Syria, Tunisia and Algeria. There were whole families, single women, and widows with children, single men and unaccompanied minors; the latter mostly teenagers aged 13–17. Among the detainees there were some who were highly educated and spoke English well. No-one, including DIMIA and ACM, seemed to know what would happen to us or, if they did, they didn't tell us.

Generally speaking, about 80 to 85 per cent of detainees had experienced the devastating effects of war and were traumatised because of losing close friends or family members. As well, there were many who experienced fear, persecution, hunger and the loss of homes and livelihoods and some would suffer imprisonment and torture. I started to discuss these tragedies and sad stories with Father Tom Atherton [a Uniting Church minister at Woomera] in the hope that he might influence DIMIA and the ACM officers to show some compassion and respect for people who had suffered so much. Above all, we should be treated humanely. Since I had lived and studied in the United Kingdom for my PhD I knew about fair treatment as part of the Western style of life.

Father Tom Atherton did his best but there didn't seem to be any improvement in our treatment. We were looked on as ignorant and illiterate—even undesirable people who shouldn't have come to Australia. I tried to be patient, behave myself and obey the rules as far as possible. I encouraged others to do the same but waiting and waiting was too much for many of them. They started to lose hope for the future. With such traumatised backgrounds they were in no shape to endure the harsh environment of Woomera detention centre. In June 2000 about 500 detainees broke out of the centre after tearing down the fence. They marched through the main street of Woomera carrying banners and shouting, 'We want freedom.' Some of them told reporters that they had been treated like criminals and that they had been held too long without information, legal rights or outside contact. After returning to the centre the outrage of the detainees started to build up again and erupted once more with the riots in August. (pers. comm.)

I concentrated my adult teaching efforts on the Afghanis in the India compound and the others in the main compound. Margota taught a group of adults in Sierra, a compound given over to those detainees unlikely to be released in the short term, if at all. I visited Sierra for the first time in mid-October and talked to some of the detainees about their situation. Some were coming up for 11 months and saw little hope for their future. They were trying to exhaust all avenues of appeal after having being rejected by their case officers. They had gained some ground, though, thanks to DIMIA manager, Tony Hamilton-Smith, who arrived in June 2000. The detainees had been screened out after the first interview. Tony listened to them and thought that some were really genuine. He advised them to organise a petition. They did and 180 people signed it. Two weeks later the interviews started again.

The tension in the main compound increased with only a few people being released—no-one knew why. We were told to be alert. Security was beefed up when six nooses were found. The biggest concern for the detainees seemed to be that they did not know about the progress of their cases. DIMIA kept them in the dark. After months of waiting, hope turned to despondency, then to despair and, finally, to a course of action not readily understood by those looking on—self-mutilation and attempted suicide. As a group, a peaceful demonstration could blow out into a full-scale riot.

We were given hostage training and shown American videos so we could cope with various types of situations that could arise in correction and detention centres. I remember being called away midway through the hostage training so I hoped I would not regret the day I had missed out on the second half.

Two of the most reliable detainees we had helping us with our teaching classes were Wahib and Morteza. We needed them because of our limited ability to communicate with the children and because they represented a cultural link. They were always punctual and very capable of looking after the children if required. Morteza, a 15-year-old, spoke Farsi and had come with his family from Iran while Wahib, a 30-year-old, and a veterinarian from Iraq, spoke Arabic and had come on his own. Their cases looked bleak as the months rolled by but it did not deter them from helping. On any spare occasion I would take Morteza for some English instruction and reading.

Wahib was always asking questions about Australia and eager to make a new life when the time came. It looked more like 'if' for both of them as most of their fellow passengers were succeeding in their visa applications. Just after my six-week contract, Margota let me know that Wahib had gained his TPV while Morteza, the most deserving person I had met, if that could be taken into consideration, had failed to have his case accepted by the Refugee Review Tribunal. We both felt very sad for him and his family.

On Thursday, 19 October, 40 detainees were released and the general mood lifted. But it was only temporary. In the next three weeks only small numbers were released and those left behind began to become even more despondent. We had more training on proper conduct inside and outside working hours. And intelligence suggested there could be the makings of another riot.

The last two weeks of my six-week contract ran by without a serious incident and I left to gather my senses. Trish hoped I could be reappointed at some stage. I did not know, though, whether I would take up another contract if offered. Doing a job was one thing but becoming embroiled in a bigger scenario was something else.

While the Government had no qualms about keeping some of these people indefinitely it seemed to me very harsh after what they had been through. Being kept in limbo was the worst part. Some had been at Woomera for nearly 12 months and had become sorrowful with their cases being rejected and having to wait long periods to exhaust all the avenues available to them.

One of the things I had realised, even after a short spell at Woomera, is that you see the asylum seekers from a different perspective. They were people desperate for a new start in life, for whatever reason. They were full of hope at the outset but gradually that hope would be whittled away if their case officer, and later the Refugee Review Tribunal, rejected their cases. And their cases could still go further than the Federal Court. Finally, once all avenues had been exhausted, there were two options: they could obtain a passport and return home (of course, at any time a detainee could opt to do this) or, if a passport were not forthcoming, try to seek asylum in another country and meanwhile stay in the detention centre. Because of their daily contact with detainees, the interpreters, welfare officers, medical staff and security officers had to cope with a whole range of problems as the detainees became more and more dysfunctional. It was little wonder that some of the staff had to be counselled as well.

TIME OUT FROM WOOMERA
(13 November 2000–4 March 2001)

The day after I left, 13 November, more than 30 Woomera detainees began a hunger strike in protest against the delays in the processing of their cases. Some of them had been there for about a year. The Department of Immigration (DIMIA) had not informed them of the progress of their applications. Not knowing what would happen seemed to unsettle them more than anything else. As the hunger strike continued into the second week, 11 detainees were taken to hospital to be rehydrated by drip-feeding. Five of them were handcuffed to prevent self-harm.

About a week later everything came to a head in the media when a nurse alleged that ACM had forced her to tear up a report of an alleged rape of a 12-year-old boy. Shortly afterwards, the Immigration Minister, Philip Ruddock, announced that there would be an inquiry into the child-abuse allegations.

Meanwhile, work was going ahead to increase the capacity of the Woomera detention centre to around 2000. Two new compounds would include demountable units, messes, education and recreational facilities for 800 detainees—all part of Phase Two.

The summer heat was relentless on those living at Woomera— the hottest, according to the weather pundits, since 1905. With very little shade, scorching heat and over-friendly flies there was no relief in this desert furnace. Along with the complaints of mismanagement, maltreatment and prison-like conditions, it was little wonder that many humanitarian groups and individuals were starting to question the necessity for these detention centres. The Government held firm though.

With increasing unrest and disturbances at Woomera, an *Encounter* program (Radio National, 21 January 2001) brought the views of a wide range of interested parties together, including those who had been released from the Woomera detention centre. One of the asylums seekers released from Woomera, Sameer, said:

> When we arrived here we were told that the Government has no interest in us and the Department of Immigration has no interest in us. They even dislike us. Even the Australian community, they dislike us. That's what we're told while we were in the detention centres. We don't want to put pressure on the Government. We do respect the Australian community and Australian people. So if they don't want to accept us they can send us to any other country . . . Just respect us and deal with us as a human being if they don't want us.

An Afghani who had been released after months at Woomera described the situation in Afghanistan:

> It was a terrible situation for us now that the interior war is there. It is based on religion. We are Muslim and we are Shiite. And the Taliban, they belong to the Sunni group. And they don't like the Shiite people. They are just very cruel. There isn't any schooling. They have shut down all the schools, industries, colleges and no education for the women and no media. They have broken down everything. They executed the prime minister of Afghanistan. And before that they hanged Hazaras. They don't like the Hazaras and that's why we had to leave because they used to come into our areas and get the young boys and used to take them to the front line of the war . . . It was the main reason why we had to leave our country. Otherwise, we had a good life there. We had orchards—apples, apricots and almonds. As well as that we had cattle. We didn't have any of the economical problems. This was the reason: just to survive. To save our life, we left the country.

In the same program, Don McMaster, who had just completed a doctoral thesis on deterrence and discrimination in the Australian Refugee Policy from 1976–1979, said he did not believe Australia should use mandatory detention for asylum seekers.

> I think it's a continuation of an attitude that's very much consistent of the White Australia Policy, where we perceive anyone as 'the other'—could have been the Jews in the 70s and 80s and into the 90s, and now we're seeing asylum seekers who are Muslim coming in. They're perceived as 'the other'. And I think that really plays on the fear that has been fairly well-instituted into the Australian psyche: a fear of invasion from the North, or, as it's been classified, the hordes from the North. And I think that is still part of an Australian attitude. It needs to change.

The family-services director for the Catholic Church's social welfare agency, Dale West, had gathered information about abuses in the Woomera detention centre, and stated that a culture of abuse had developed and that ACM was failing to exercise a duty of care for the detainees. He also made it clear that DIMIA was complicit in not delegating and ensuring responsibility for that care.

Mary Lindsay, a migration agent and contracted to review applications for refugee status, said that ACM was operating the centre like a prison. Those released from the Woomera detention centre also spoke of maltreatment and mismanagement of detainees, including that of a 10-year-old girl who had been locked up with her father and given no proper food for three days.

In December a former prime minister, Malcolm Fraser, described the Woomera detention centre as a 'hell hole'. After receiving the 2000 Human Rights Medal at a ceremony in Sydney organised by the Human Rights and Equal Opportunity Commission, he said:

The question of Woomera and refugees—or illegal migrants, as we're told they are—seems to me to be totally beyond belief when you read of the circumstances, when you know the physical character of the place. Is this really the place to put people who might be— probably are—trying to escape from absolute tyranny?

Meanwhile Immigration Minister Philip Ruddock announced an inquiry under former Foreign Affairs department chief, Philip Flood, to look at the handling of asylum seekers in detention centres. The inquiry followed findings that there were shortcomings in reporting by ACM of an alleged child abuse. At the same time, the Government was looking at a possible project for putting some women and children asylum seekers in community housing in the Woomera township. The Human Rights Commissioner, Sev Ozdowski, who inspected Woomera in late February, endorsed the Government's decision and said that it was a long overdue step and that Australia still had a long way to go.

Philip Flood's findings highlighted some of the problems in managing asylum seekers as well as drawing attention to a small number of security officers who intimidated and verbally abused detainees. He made 16 recommendations for improved manage-ment at Woomera: among them,

- DIMIA to look at the opportunities for women and children to live outside the detention centres in a more normal envi-ronment;
- ACM to improve the physical conditions at the Woomera detention centre; improved training for ACM staff to promote more humane treatment of asylum seekers;
- DIMIA to reduce the processing time for asylum seekers receiving primary decisions for temporary protection visas; and for
- DIMIA to conduct quarterly reviews of ACM's per-formance.

Although going a long way to address the shortcomings of

detention centres, the Flood report stopped short of denouncing them altogether as suitable places to put asylum seekers.

One of the positive outcomes of the Flood report and other findings was that various refugee advocacy and human rights groups would be able to inspect facilities and services at detention centres.

I could not go to the media because of signing a secrecy agreement with ACM but I wrote to our Federal Member of Parliament and Speaker of the House of Representatives, Neil Andrew. I told him I felt strongly about the delays in processing the cases and suggested, in any case, there should be a ceiling on the length of time spent in the detention centres. Detainees could be released under a special bond where they had to report every so often to a government agency. I also suggested some avenues of investigation to improve ways in which refugees could come to Australia without resorting to assistance by organised smuggling rackets. The letter was passed on to Philip Ruddock, the Minister for Immigration and Multicultural Affairs, and a reply came back about four months later.

Just before starting another contract as an education officer, this time for six months, I had an opportunity to spend half a day with about 25 people who had been released from Woomera on 1 March 2001. Through arrangements with the Department of Human Services and the Coalition for Justice for Refugees, the temporary visa holders spent their first night in a backpackers' hostel. Two Farsi and Arabic interpreters accompanied them to the State Housing Trust office area, where Nabil, an Arabic-speaking employee, spoke to them about renting houses or units. Afterwards, we made our way to the Commonwealth Bank so they could open an account and receive a temporary bank card to access a first payment. For most it was the first time they had operated an automatic teller machine.

Then they registered with the Medicare and Centrelink offices. The interpreters led them to the market where I thought we would be having lunch. What a great idea! Instead, the interpreters parted company and told me that the visa holders would get their own lunch and find their way around. Only two persons of the group seemed to speak passable English. What a learning process ahead!

To assist in the settlement of visa holders, various community sectors had come together to form the Coalition for Justice for Refugees: they were concerned that refugees granted temporary protection visas would be denied many of the services available to other refugees.

Farhad Noori was the coordinator of settlement services and, as a refugee himself from Iran, had been moved by the way Australian citizens helped him. He welcomed asylum seekers and helped them find accommodation and employment. Working at the Australian Refugee Association (ARA) offices, he and others were committed to helping them settle and find employment. They also referred them to other agencies such as St Vincent de Paul, Salvation Army and Wesley Uniting Mission for assistance with household items and clothing.

On 4 March 2001, the day before I was due to start my six-month contract, Minister Philip Ruddock met a group of Woomera residents, including the entire Woomera Area Board, to discuss proposals to 'release' 25 women and children into the community while their applications were being processed. Officers would act as 'house parents' and the detainees would be able to shop and take part in community events. No men would be allowed to take part in this trial and teenage boys would not be classified as children. Mr Ruddock responded to questions raised by residents concerning the justification of the trial, health, education and security issues, and the impact on tourism.

WOOMERA UNFOLDS
(5 March–31 May 2001)

'We're moving away from the six-week contracts,' said Vic, the human resources manager. 'We'd prefer the one-year contract so as to give opportunities for families to come. The longer contracts would be better for everyone.'

I thought I wouldn't survive a one-year spell at Woomera so I replied, 'How about six months?'

'Yes, we can do that. When would you like to start?'

So, with that brief phone conversation I started on 5 March 2001. It was still hot, though I had missed the very hot summer for which I was thankful. Liz, my wife, would join me in three weeks' time. She had resigned from her position as a registered nurse and was looking forward to a well-earned rest.

If I had any illusions that the next six months were going to be like the previous six-week spell it soon disappeared. In November 2000, there had been about 250 detainees with only a handful of children —making life relatively easy in terms of teaching. Intelligence reports were now indicating that this could blow out to 2000 with the expected arrival of further boatloads.

I boarded the tiny nineteen-seater turboprop aircraft at Adelaide airport. Bent double, we made our way to our respective seats. Harold, the clinical psychologist, was in front of me and quipped, 'They should sell these to the Third World countries.' Someone behind me agreed. An hour later we landed at Olympic Dam and met David, our driver. Peter, a new teacher from Brisbane, was also there.

As we approached the detention centre the four-metre high

palisade fence topped by razor wire was pervasive. The razor wire had been installed after about 500 detainees had broken out of the previous fence, now the internal fence, in June 2000. The galvanised all-steel product of the palisade fence resisted cutting and ramming, I was told. And the helical coil of razor wire with needle-sharp barbs at ten-centimetre intervals was superior to flat tape or barbed-wire products; heavy bolt cutters were needed to cut it. The barbed tape had originally been developed over 20 years earlier for use in Vietnam; it has been used successfully in military and correctional facilities since. But there was no word of it being used in a processing centre. Could it withstand the onslaught of determined asylum seekers? There would be no absconding, it seemed, if all else failed. The curtain had come down on all hope. I was wrong though—three months later seven detainees did escape.

The double-sided five-metre high palisade gate dwarfed us as we went into the Woomera detention centre. In the administrative block we met Trish, the programs leader, Sharon, a recreational officer, and Margota and Liz, the two teachers who had stayed over summer. There were only a few people wandering around the compounds, though the board in the operations room showed the numbers of different nationalities—45 Iraqis, 100 Iranians and 225 Afghanis.

Margota and Liz would stay with us a few more days so we could find our feet. The next day I started teaching mathematics to about 20 young boys and girls. In the compound areas there were new faces everywhere. Some of those who had been there more than one year had been shifted to the Sierra compound. Others who had been there the previous year had been sent to Port Hedland for possible deportation. Morteza, our assistant teacher, had been one of them. As the day wore on Peter had that glazed shell-shocked appearance common to new appointees. Margota brought us up to date with the latest on Woomera centre—everything was changing—rules, policies, the scrutinising by visitors and tougher action on any kind of child abuse. One of the assistant detainee teachers had cuffed a boy in class and had been reported. I had noticed that this was quite a common practice by parents, to bring children into line. The teacher had been suspended pending a police investigation. I was sure that even if the teacher were reinstated he wouldn't be too keen to teach again.

At 4 pm we had our weekly programs-team meeting in which Trish as chairperson welcomed the newcomers and thanked everyone for a week's hard work. She reminded us that all staff had access to the new set of upgraded policies and we were to become familiar with them, in particular the policy regarding the *Child Protection Act*. Also a reminder that if we reported to FAYS (Family and Youth Services of South Australia) about a case of alleged child abuse we had to let DIMIA and ACM know as well. Monthly reports had to be handed in and daily statistics were important. And then there were questions from Jamal, the Arabic interpreter, about the difficulties of detainees obtaining permission to obtain documents in support of their cases.

I was eager to find out more about what was going on this time and resolved to have more contact with the detainees and staff. Everyone seemed to have their own perspective on the asylum seekers—DIMIA, the various ACM staff, the Federal Government, the refugee action groups and, of course, the public. Did anyone have a full picture of what was going on? I doubted if anyone or any organisation could or would know the full story. Being at the grassroots level, though, the programs staff were in an ideal place to gain some detailed knowledge.

Induction, the next day, covered a whole host of topics. Bernice, the medical doctor, talked about the importance of taking precautions for preventing infectious diseases—a real concern with the detainees. Then there were talks on intelligence reporting, policies and procedures for the high risk assessment team (HRAT), occupation, health and safety, child protection, reporting, referral, communications, the importance of attitudes and values and so on. But we did not have to put the riot gear on.

Following the induction Margota and Liz put us in the picture. It was nothing like the old days. The workload seemed enormous with a six-hour contact time plus the supervision of detainee teachers and preparation of material for them, daily records of attendance, special forms for the unaccompanied minors and payment sheets for the assistant teachers. And we had to spend A$50,000 on ordering books for the library by next Monday. An expected 300 more boat people were due in the next week.

On Friday, Peter and I held a teachers' meeting. We met our assistant detainee teachers, Ali, Yusef, Musa, Tawakoli, Hussain, Maher, Mehdi and Salem. All were keen to have English teaching themselves and practical aids for their classes, such as conversational exercises and tapes. They were reasonably fluent in English as well as speaking Arabic or Persian Farsi or Dari Farsi from Afghanistan. We agreed to have a meeting every Friday morning so as to 'empower' the teachers, as Peter put it.

The following Monday we saw no sign of any teachers. Salem and Maher had been held up in the India compound with no-one to escort them across and so Peter and I shuttled back and forth with four classes in four separate rooms. Fortunately, we kept everyone busy with colouring cards for Margota's farewell the next day. Liz had already gone, having completed her three months' teaching contract.

The 13–17-year-old girls were particularly adept at drawing and colouring. They were a lively bunch—Bunin, Shaima, Gulshan, Betul, Sarah, Sahar, Nazeerah, Maryam and Tayyaba. Shaima from Afghanistan was the most outspoken and had an excellent command of English.

Shaima belonged to the minority ethnic group, the Hazaras, who had suffered brutally at the hands of the Taliban. She told us that the Taliban had come to their small family farm one day and demanded that their father hand over their land. Shaima's father refused to give the land so the Taliban had come one night and taken him away. Her mother, fearful for the fate of her five daughters and two sons, fled to her cousin's home. That family was also in fear and decided to escape with the aid of a smuggler. Shaima's mother urged her daughter to go with the family. They had fled Afghanistan in late 2000 and eventually boarded a fishing boat in Indonesia. After a six-day voyage, on which there had been no food and precious little water, an Australian naval vessel had intercepted them.

In the afternoon there were about 20 13–17-year-old boys, many of them unaccompanied minors, for social studies. They settled down well as we talked about Australia. I spoke as slowly as possible and used the more proficient English speakers to translate when necessary.

The next day I took the girls on an imaginary shopping expedition to the supermarket. We had a lot of fun as we discussed some of the items and how much we would have to pay. Then Javed, a new assistant, and I took on more than 20 exuberant youngsters, aged eight to 12, for mathematics and then the 13–17-year-old boys for a lesson on travelling in Australia. We covered distances and how long it would take to go by car from one place to the other, as well as fuel costs.

After the children's classes I had a chance to talk to Haman, a 31-year-old Iranian, who was keen to help out in the teaching program. He seemed a sincere and earnest person with a strong desire to do something useful with his life. Following graduation in Iran, with a diploma in engineering, he had done his military service before looking for work in his field. After a lot of searching, he was finally employed in a temporary position. He had lived in a small town where some of the local Muslims regarded him as an infidel because he did not participate fully in the prayer times at the mosque.

Haman had become so frustrated with the job situation and other matters that he decided to leave Iran in April 1999. He bought a false passport and travelled to Kuching, Malaysia and then went to Hong Kong with the intention of travelling on to Canada.

He was detained by the authorities in Hong Kong, however, and spent four months in jail. During that time there were riots in Teheran University and some students were killed. He was greatly upset by these events and wrote two strongly worded articles for magazines. After the articles were published he was advised not to return to Iran. He was released and made his way back to Malaysia, and then on to Indonesia, before leaving on a boat for Australia. He hoped to have an opportunity to make a new life for himself here.

The farewell dinner for Margota was a convivial affair in the Woomera Returned and Services League Bowling Club. Margota was in good spirits and the red wine flowed freely. Her account of an overnight stay in a nudist camp in the Barossa Valley had everyone in fits of laughter. All admired her creative ability, enthusiasm and warmth in teaching. And she had a good sense of humour that helped her to cope with the difficult teaching environment. No, she wouldn't come back; she and her husband would go to China and teach English there.

People from a human rights organisation visited us on Thursday, 15 March; the operations manager accompanied them. The children were engrossed in their studies when they appeared. We told them about the classes—the 5–7s, the 8–12s, 13–17-year-old boys and 13–17-year-old girls, and also the kindergarten, library and computer room. If they had come a little earlier they would have stepped into a classroom full of teenage girls crying. Thursday, being a release day, triggered this outpouring of emotion. Shaima had explained that they were away from their homeland, in a strange environment and there was no knowing what would become of them. I tried my best to give some hope and they seemed to respond.

In the coming weeks and months there were many more visits by human rights, refugee and other concerned organisations; they usually breezed in and out in a day. It was 'hit or miss' whether you saw them. It seemed that they had very little time to make detailed observations and to talk about problems with the detainees. How could they make proper assessments? Perhaps they had skills beyond my understanding. In the six months that followed I spoke briefly to three groups and responded to questions for about five to ten minutes on each occasion.

The president of the Australian Council of Civil Liberties, Terry Gorman, put his finger on the pulse when he called on the Federal Government to establish an inspector-general position to monitor detention centres on a weekly basis and report to Parliament. He said:

> It is clearly time that there is an outside body that not only monitors what happens in detention centres but can go there regularly with no notice and get in and see independently what is going on.

In the main compound I met a couple of fellows who had fled from Ghazni, Afghanistan. Their relatives had had to sell land to pay the smugglers. From Quetta in Pakistan they had flown to Singapore and on to Jakarta, where they were bundled into a van and hidden in the jungle for two weeks before being taken to the coast. There they had boarded a small Indonesian vessel that would take them to Ashmore Reef.

This was typical of many stories that I would hear over the next few months. I encouraged them both to come along to the English classes.

The new centre manager, Peter McIntosh, was keen to have a proper computer centre running in the main compound. He had the maintenance staff prepare a transportable unit opposite the library. Six Pentium computers were installed and we were in business. I spread the word that I was looking for someone to manage the computer centre. The next day Amir, who had been a computer operator in Iran, turned up. I hired him at one dollar an hour—all that we were allowed to pay detainees. In reality, the detainees were awarded points that were exchanged for goods such as phonecards and cigarettes. Amir, along with Jalil, our library assistant, started classes on 26 March. The teenage girls were rather giggly and overly enthusiastic but gradually Amir and Jalil calmed them down and after they had been taught some basics on how to operate a computer they started on a typing program. The young boys were too boisterous so we sent them out. We would try again the next day after drawing up a roster.

The next day the 8–12-year-old boys stormed the computers before we even had a chance to put the roster into effect. They jostled, pushed and even punched their way to the front. The computer craze had truly started. Jalil and Amir turned most of the boys away but not before one of them was mysteriously struck on the back. The boy reported the incident; he alleged that Jalil had hit him. Jalil said he had not touched anyone and that the boy must have fallen against a piece of metal jutting out from the donga. Jalil was stood down pending an inquiry. We had lost our librarian and computer assistant. His wife, Sima, and two teenage girls, Maryam and Afsaneh, couldn't believe what had happened. Jalil had been a teacher in Iran and like all the assistant teachers he had been through the training program in child protection.

We organised computer classes for the adult men and women in the afternoon, trying our best to share the computer time out between Iraqis, Iranians and Afghanis. With only six computers, Amir tried to roster everyone as fairly as possible without causing conflict between the nations.

Zeyad, a computer graphics designer from Iraq, offered his help in running classes for the adults. They were a huge success as Zeyad explained the basics before launching into Corel Draw and Adobe Photoshop programs. We could not cope with the demand so we put on some evening classes. Zeyad valued the support of Ali Akber, an unaccompanied minor from Afghanistan, who spoke English and quickly mastered both computer programs. Ali became our assistant computer teacher for both children and adults.

Meanwhile, we were keen to find someone who could take the

boys and girls for some sporting activities. Amir, the computer operator, suggested his cousin Aziz, also from Iran. He was the ideal person—keen on fitness and soccer. We hired him and most days he jogged to the classroom, sometimes with a couple of soccer balls under his arms and wearing a broad smile.

Aziz told me his story. He had left behind his wife and nine-year-old daughter. His intention was to secure a safe haven in another country and later send for them. This would be a common theme for many detainees. Aziz's wife was injured by pieces of shrapnel in a market place when an Iraqi plane bombed the area. She could walk only with difficulty and suffered a lot from head-aches. As a worker of a sugar-plantation company he helped organise demonstrations to protest about the low wages. In his spare time he also distributed Mujahideen pamphlets that informed people about the extent of corruption in the Government. This had been dangerous work and Aziz had known what would happen if discovered. Many young people, including two of his cousins, had already been executed.

In April 2000 Aziz helped organise others to close the streets leading to the company building. The workers had been very upset with working conditions so it had been easy to arrange the demonstration. The Sepah secret police were called in and, after they had used tear gas and made some arrests, the demonstrators dispersed. After that demonstration, Aziz was fired and so he started to drive a taxi. He still helped to distribute pamphlets exposing the Government and once two Mujahideen members assisting him had been arrested. Aziz managed to escape. The authorities, though, were looking for the third person and Aziz knew he had to leave Iran. Aziz and his cousin, Amir, who had his own reasons for leaving Iran, moved to Shiraz, where they obtained passports. They flew to Malaysia from Shiraz, and made contact with a smuggling ring.

Escaping from Iran had been one thing; another was to make it to Australia. Aziz and Amir would experience some of the many hazards in being smuggled out to Ashmore Reef or Christmas Island. Aziz had already lost one of his suitcases in Kuala Lumpur. They paid a smuggler to help them but he disappeared. They tried again with another smuggler. This time arrangements were made to send them to Indonesia by boat. When they arrived at the coast for boarding they were told to lie down to avoid being detected by the regular coast guard patrols. Just before dawn they were told to wade out to a boat filled with coconuts. The water swirled around their necks as they were taken on board. There were about 35 men and standing room only. Suddenly, the boat struck a rock and everyone fell into the sea. Fortunately, they were still close to shore and managed to drag themselves on to the beach with whatever baggage they could retrieve. They walked back to their coastal pick-up point, and after three hours they were exhausted as well as hungry and thirsty. The smuggler who had arranged the rendezvous heard what had happened and returned by car. He promised to prepare a seaworthy boat. They hid near the beach to await the arrival of two boats the following evening. This time when they left they hid under a sheet of plastic aboard their boat and nearly choked with the exhaust fumes. The engine broke down and they lost sight of the other boat at night. Having repaired the engine, the boat moved on and came across the other boat. Its engine had also seized. It was raining heavily but the seawater that began to come into the boat was a greater concern. Shivering, they baled continuously until the next morning.

They were exhausted but happy. They towed the other boat and after four days drew near to the coast of Sumatra. A boat approached them and they were taken to a beach where they disembarked. The beach was like quicksand. Some villagers met them and offered a foul type of cordial. Even though they were very thirsty, some could not swallow the drink. They paid one of the people to hire a vehicle for them. While they waited, more and more people gathered around and they became afraid. Finally, a truck arrived and they clambered aboard the back and hid under a fibrous sheet. They arrived in Medan, the capital of Sumatra, and stayed a night in a hotel. The following day they flew to Jakarta where they stayed for five days before travelling by bus to Bali. Then they travelled to an island where members of the smuggling ring were waiting. The smugglers took them to the beach by car and, after spending a night there, a boat picked them up and transferred them to a larger vessel. Some were put near the engine, which was smoky and noisy. The men mostly stayed on deck while the children and women were confined to a dirty cabin.

After two days at sea they found out that the young sea captain had lost his way. They ran out of drinking water and began to dehydrate. Fighting nearly broke out because of the lack of water. Someone who had some knowledge of sailing checked the maps and with the aid of a compass was able to approximately determine their position. He charted a new course for Ashmore Reef. After another day an Australian airplane spotted them and then Australian boats guided them to Ashmore Reef, where they stayed for eight days before going on to Darwin by ferry.

After two more days they were in the Woomera detention centre. They had survived their smuggling experience but the most difficult hurdle lay ahead.

Like most other Iranians, DIMIA had screened them out after the first interview. The screening out effectively meant that they could not continue with the second and third interviews that were required for a primary decision by the case officer.

I was always on the lookout for assistant teachers as some would be released and others would quit because teaching was not for them. Often it was because they had become so depressed after being rejected by their DIMIA-appointed case officer or the Refugee Review Tribunal. To their credit, detainees such as Jalil and Salem still stayed on to help, despite having their cases turned down. Maybe they could see that it was far better for their sanity to remain active and involved in something else than to be consumed by despair. They were under no delusion, though, that helping out in the teaching program would earn any points with DIMIA.

The teachers were paid one dollar an hour—just enough for a few cigarettes. Most earned one or two dollars a day for their teaching efforts. Amir would earn the maximum of eight dollars for managing the computer room. There were other opportunities to earn this 'pocket money', such as working in the kitchen, cleaning out the toilets, gardening and helping in the warehouse.

Peter and I were the only teachers for an increasing number of detainees as more boat people arrived, mostly from Afghanistan. We decided to split up the children and the adults. Peter would take responsibility for the 13–17-year-old boys and girls as well as the adult women. I would try to handle the youngsters, 5–7s and 8–12s, and the adult men for English and Australian life skills. In addition I would look after the computer services, the library, kindergarten and the daily statistics.

We had four or five women looking after the kindergarten children. One of them, Zahra, a 27-year-old mother from Afghanistan had arrived in Australia with her three-month-old daughter, Omulbani. Her husband had come on a previous boat and had obtained a temporary protection visa. As Hazaras and Shiites, they had suffered persecution under the Taliban. Somehow, though, her story did not gel with her case officer and her application was rejected. On hearing the news she became suicidal and had to be helped by Alley, the social welfare officer, to cope with her rejection. After a while she gained some composure, becoming a favourite in the kindergarten and always helping out despite her own misfortunes. One of the liaison officers, Dan, took a special interest in her baby, Omulbani, and was able to provide the usual powders, shampoos and nappies that babies need. The only difficulty Dan had was remembering the baby's name. On one occasion he resorted to calling her *Omul banana* and Zahra burst into laughter.

Dan, as a liaison officer, had one of the busiest jobs in the centre. His duties included maintaining records of residents, supervising toilet cleaning and laundry workers, and controlling the issue of clothing items, cleaning and hygiene products, as well as welfare and property requests. In the main compound, 30 or more detainees would often assemble in a disorderly queue outside the liaison office for their requests. On one occasion, a man, who spoke limited English, approached me about his wife who would not join the queue for some personal items. I spoke to Dan about her need and he was happy to help out.

Peter seemed to settle in well with the teenagers and women. He was an irrepressible actor with a deft sense of hyperbole and an extraordinary range of antics and clowning in his repertoire. Apart from missing out on an acting career he would have made an enjoyable politician—a rarity these days. He was an experienced teacher of English as a second language. The children and women took to him and enjoyed his friendly teaching as well as his performances.

Salem, a 50-year-old teacher of English from Iraq, was happy to take a beginners' class while I concentrated on those who already spoke some English. Salem had faced persecution as a Shiite and had left behind his wife and two sons aged eight and 11. His brother, also a teacher, and father of six children, had been arrested and accused of being a member of the Al-Dawaa Islamic Party; he had been executed in 1985.

Salem felt responsible for looking after the children and he married his brother's widow in 1988. After the Gulf War in 1991, the suffering of the Shiites in Basra increased because they were held responsible for the events that had occurred in Iraq. Through his teaching, Salem tried to support the students as much as possible. In January 1995 the headmaster of the school asked him to go to the Al-Maakal security department. There, they questioned him about his past life and associations. He was beaten and accused of working against the Al-Baa'th Party. His family put up bail and he was released. Fearing the same fate as his brother would befall him, his wife advised him not to return to Basra and to leave his job. He did return, however, and found to his dismay that he was not welcomed back at the school. He resigned and worked with another brother in a small furniture shop in Karbala. The Karbala authorities arrested and beat Shiites, as in Basra. Salem decided to leave Iraq and, with the aid of smugglers, went to Jordan before flying to Malaysia and then on by boat to Indonesia and finally Australia.

There were about 25 men, mostly Iraqis, who came to the advanced English class. I made the class as practical as possible by setting up a range of conversational scenarios, such as making an appointment with the doctor, booking a room for the night and answering the phone. After a practice session with the whole class and a few people I had picked out, they practised among themselves. We then talked about Australia and introduced various life skills, such as driving a car, shopping at the supermarket, using credit cards, paying bills, buying a mobile phone, looking for a place to rent and rental agreements, and taking care of our health. They enjoyed themselves and for a brief moment forgot about their Woomera woes.

One of the detainees, a 27-year-old from Iran, usually came in late and sat at the back of the classroom. His shoulder-length hair made him stand out from the rest. He listened intently without saying much. His dark eyes were friendly but sorrowful. He reminded me of a drawing of Jesus I had once seen. After one of the classes he approached me and introduced himself as Bijan. He was keen to help teach and I replied that we still needed assistant teachers.

'What would you like to teach?' I asked.

'I would like to take classes in meditation and hypnotism,' Bijan responded.

His reply threw me a little. I thought for a moment and said that would be good but we had better call the classes 'meditation and relaxation'. I was happy to give him a go and said I would arrange a classroom. There would be separate classes for children and adults. I was sure Bijan was no Svengali and it certainly could not do any harm in this type of environment. I talked it over with Pam, a newly appointed recreational officer, and she agreed to keep an eye on the classes.

Bijan said that he had become a Christian after leaving the Islamic faith four years earlier. He was not baptised, as he had been too scared to go to church in Iran and Syria. In 1998, he commenced a course of study called scientific sports, about yoga, meditation, Zen, hypnotism and hypnoanalysis. Bijan studied in Iran and then went to Syria to work and also continued his study by correspondence. He returned to Iran in January 2001 to study a subject that he could not do by correspondence. During one of the sessions he presented a paper comparing Christianity with Islam. Although he had not expressed his own views, his fellow students nevertheless interpreted his comments as an admission that he had abandoned Islam. After class, one of the students said he was from the Government and that Bijan had to go to Basij for questioning. There, he was accused of rejecting Islam and of being a *mortad*, for which the penalty was death. Bijan was released under a guarantee from his brother that he would appear in court should the authorities want to question him further. Shortly afterwards, Bijan left illegally, on an Iraqi passport arranged by his brother.

Two others who were keen to assist in teaching English were Shahin, and his expectant wife, Samira. Shahin was like a breath of fresh air with his slim boyish appearance belying his mature approach to life. As a 25-year-old graduate from an Iranian university he spoke fluent English. His hope and belief for a new life in Australia were strong. As a compassionate man who quickly appreciated the complexity of the legal situation for Iranians held in detention, he would do much for them in the future. He had held an important office before his escape from Iran. Samira's father had been involved in anti-government political activities which caused some serious problems for Shahin in his workplace. There had

been no other option but to sell a house to provide money for passports, travel to Malaysia and for the smugglers.

Shahin and Samira went by ferry from Penang to Belawan in
Sumatra. From Medan in Sumatra they flew to Jakarta and then to
Bali before catching a ferry to Lombok Island to meet their contact
with the smuggling organisation. As soon as they disembarked
from the ferry they were put under house arrest for three months.
The 'smuggler' had informed the police and had escaped with
their money. They were given contaminated water to drink and
little food. Samira contracted typhoid, and being pregnant added to
the seriousness of this. Fortunately, they managed to escape to
Mataram where they established contact with another smuggler.
They boarded a boat for Ashmore Reef from Lombok. On seeing
the boat their hearts sank. The small wooden fishing vessel seemed
on its last legs—a far cry from Samira's hopes of a commercial ship.

'Everyone saw death before our eyes,' Samira said later. 'We
had no money left, we had no choice.' Somehow they arrived
safely after a harrowing four-day voyage; it was a bitter-sweet
encounter with Australia as they remembered their families and
friends back in Iran.

Other accounts of the voyages from Indonesian coastal ports to
Ashmore Reef in over-crowded, unseaworthy boats would make
anyone think twice about putting their life in peril. Some of the
teenage girls told how they had been packed like sardines on a 15-
metre boat. The waves had lashed at them all night, with everyone
screaming. They all thought they would be swept overboard. There
had been no food except biscuits and a glass of oily water. And no
toilets. Arriving at Ashmore Reef had been arrival into paradise.

The sea voyage was the last leg of a harrowing sequence of
events for children. Knowing their personal backgrounds and especially their traumatic experiences it would not be surprising for
them to have behavioural problems. A small number of children—
usually about 10 per cent—aged 5–12, did not come to classes.

Some had withdrawn from contact with other children. Some had come initially and not again. We referred those who persistently refused to come to the psychologist. There were a few children who did come and whose behavioural problems were such that we sometimes referred them to counselling.

There were two sisters, Negira, aged 11, and Samina, aged nine, who came to class initially and then withdrew. I tried to encourage them to come but they preferred to play in the dirt surrounding the classrooms. I informed the psychologist, who tried to convince them that activities in the school were a better option. They came to classes for a short time and sadly then withdrew again. Their brothers, Alamdar and Muntazer, showed a similar response to long-term detention. They showed great promise in the classroom at first and then 'switched off'. One of Alamdar's drawings showed a Taliban fighter holding the severed head of a young child with whom Alamdar had been playing. The children had come with their mother, Roqia, and uncle from Oruzgan province in central Afghanistan to the Woomera centre in December 2000. The Taliban had persecuted the family, they said, because they were Shiite Muslims as well as belonging to the Hazara ethnic minority. The children's father, Ali Bakhtiari, had come a year earlier and been detained in Western Australia's Port Hedland detention centre. Ali Bakhtiari was released after ten months but did not learn about his family's fate until about eight months later.

The Family and Youth Services (FAYS), as part of the Department of Human Services in South Australia, was responsible for investigating any kind of child abuse, whether emotional, physical, sexual or neglect. Ironically, the only case of significance that was brought before FAYS was the one involving alleged sexual abuse the previous year.

A strong case could be mounted for emotional abuse of all children in detention, especially for those staying more than six months. Not much was said at first. Slowly the tide turned and more people spoke out against children being in detention and

Drawings by Alamdar Bakhtiari

suffering emotional abuse. Many of the children would witness hunger strikes and self-mutilation by other detainees. According to concerned leaders in the community, the children had committed no crime and it was a breach of the United Nations Convention on the Rights of the Child ratified by Australia in 1990.

According to child protection legislation in South Australia, emotional abuse is of concern if the child has suffered, or is likely to suffer, psychological injury detrimental to the child's wellbeing; or the child's psychological development is in jeopardy (Children's Protection Act, 1993). FAYS practice guidelines refer to the repeated, continual behaviour or ongoing attitude on the part of the parent/caregiver towards the child.

The caregiver, of course, was the Federal Government through DIMIA. Two types of behaviour, described by FAYS, and particularly relevant to detainees with respect to emotional abuse, concerned: isolation—cutting the child off from normal social experience, preventing the development of interpersonal skills and disallowing spontaneous fun and enjoyment; and corruption—teaching the child socially deviant patterns of behaviour. The latter could be redefined to predisposing the child to socially deviant patterns of behaviour through instituting a prison-like environment.

All of these developments were of no avail to Negira, Samina, Alamdar and Muntazer. They remained in detention for more than a year and the only way to recognise their plight was a tragic one. On Australian Day, 26 January 2002, Mazar Ali, their uncle, would make front pages across Australia and the world by climbing the fence and plunging into the razor wire (*see* front and back cover). He survived but with many stitches to his face, stomach, arms and legs. Mazar Ali's protest nearly cost him his life, a life he was willing to let go in order to draw attention to the plight of his sister and his nephews and nieces.

Zahra, an Afghani girl, also showed signs of detention stress. No-one was really sure of her age, including Zahra herself who thought she might be 12 years old. At the beginning of her detention stay she was enthusiastic about her lessons and always turned up to class with a smile and headscarf faithfully in place. As the months rolled by, though, she became listless and withdrawn. There were occasions when she returned to her former bright self and turned up to class. But the detention syndrome prevailed. About a year later, in the Easter protest of 2002, the outside world caught a snapshot of her emotional distress as one of the Australian protesters hugged her outside the razor wire.

Each child was supposed to have a file. While nothing appeared on most files a few were full of reports. One of these was of an eight-year-old lad who threw regular tantrums if he did not get his own way. He was hyperactive and always fighting with his class-mates, even the girls. In front of a computer he was quiet, except once when he should have given his computer to a 13-year-old girl on the changeover. He refused to budge and then all of a sudden he started swinging punches. It got worse—he kicked and swore Australian style. I came running when I heard the commotion and immediately pulled him away from the girl, taking care not to use any unnecessary force or I would be in trouble too. I checked the girl to see if she had been harmed in any way and then tried to pacify the lad.

These incidents can come back to haunt you so I wrote up an incident report. Since it was a fight involving children I did not think I would have to report it to FAYS. The ACM intelligence officer thought otherwise. To check this, I rang the Department of Human Services in Adelaide and spoke to someone who said that the incident was not child abuse involving an adult, and that the ACM social welfare officer should handle the case.

The children loved drawing and we were fortunate to have Sadiq, a 25-year old signwriter and self-taught artist from Afghanistan. Sadiq liked poetry, writing, painting and calligraphy. As an art teacher he gently guided the children in their efforts, showing by example more than by procedure. The children would watch first of all as something took form from his free-flowing penmanship or brushwork. We marvelled at what the children could accomplish under his direction. Sadiq's own sketches were incredible, often capturing the poignant suffering of the Afghani people or the brutality of the Taliban.

Sadiq had worked as a sign-writer in Afghanistan for about ten years. He was given work by government departments, United Nations officers, the city council and the Taliban. Sadiq came from a Hazara background and it was well-known that the Taliban were

Artwork by Sadiq.
Top right is Hafizah's card.

waging a relentless and brutal campaign against the Hazaras. As well as being careful about his true identity he pretended to be a Sunni Muslim when the Taliban were around. He feared that it would be just a matter of time before the Taliban arrested him and so he planned an escape. His wife wanted to accompany him with their three children. Sadiq decided that the route out of Afghanistan would be too dangerous so he left his family behind in the care of his parents.

Somehow I had inherited the editing and publishing of the detainee newsletter entitled *Hope*. Peter, the ACM manager, was keen for it to come out fortnightly with contributions mainly from detainees. Shahin was willing to help collect and type the articles, so in our first one-page effort we encouraged people to contribute messages, poems, short stories, light-hearted information, impressions on arriving in Australia and anything else of interest. Articles started to come in from a few detainees and we included them in the next few issues of *Hope*, provided of course they were cleared by DIMIA. The articles were translated into Arabic and Farsi. Two were even approved for release in Woomera's community newspaper, the *Gibber Gabber*. They were the following:

PEACE

Peace is a very nice word. It is clean, like a feather, light like the moon, and calm like the night.

How good it would be if all the people around the world could live in peace.

I didn't see peace in my country, but I heard about it. I know what it means.

I am surprised when I see people living in peace. Whenever I see them, I say to myself, 'How lucky they are!'

At that time, I pray to God and say that I hope peace will come to my country too, because I am a girl who has never spent her life in peace, like millions of girls in my country, Afghanistan.

Since then I have seen people with problems and I have seen people die in front of me without any reason.

I have seen children lose their parents, I have seen women become widows and I have seen houses destroyed.

I saw war in my country all the time and I never heard any good news there. That is why I abhor that kind of life.

Afghanistan's girls also want to fulfil their dreams and live in a peaceful place like others do.

We want a bright future and to live the way we want as women.

It is our right but unfortunately we don't have any rights in Afghanistan.

I hope that peace will come to Afghanistan and that all women will be able to fulfil their hopes.

Geeta

A SEA STORY

Happy are those who feel the need for God. The angels in heaven will watch over them.

Our worn out ship was sailing on an endless ocean towards Australia. We were passengers, each one with an interesting story from their past.

We felt that God was with us and in each cell of our body.

The ship disturbed the tranquillity of the sea with its noisy engine. Even the fish seemed to be surprised about us being aboard.

Then there was the unpleasant news that our water was running out and the ship's rudder had broken.

The passengers became restless and impatient as the weather became warmer. Drinking water was distributed and the people raised their hands in prayer.

God was with us and because of our need we felt close to him.

There was an old man sitting calmly in the corner and staring at some point on the boat. Maybe he was thinking about his wife and children who did not have a guardian or maybe he was thinking about death.

A child took the old man's water bottle and, in a confused state, the old man took it back. But then he hugged the child and held the water bottle to the mouth of the child.

What a beautiful moment living by the golden rule to love others. You must do the same thing to others, as you would want them to do to you.

I no longer insisted on looking after my water ration. The engine sound was now like the best music. I took my own water bottle and approached the old man. I did not say a word nor did he say anything. He sipped and smiled, his eyes were shining—perhaps he was thinking of his children.

Then the commotion on board increased and a boat came toward us. Yes, we were saved. The old man laughed and kissed the young child slowly. 'My wife and children will sleep comfortably because we are alive,' he said.

Happy are those who mourn because they will be comforted and happy are those who are kind and forgiving because they will receive forgiveness from others.

Hajatollah

Some articles described their anguish, some were poetical and some were light-hearted.

Iraj, a 36-year-old from Iran, who despaired of ever being released, wrote:

The best moment of a caged bird is getting its freedom.

Oh, my God, I beseech and call on you from the whirlpool of sorrows to hear my voice and listen to my groaning and assist my wife.

Mehrzad, also from Iran, looked for meaning in life:

The flute of my mind is blowing
The world is rocking
Is it a creature that is blowing?
So who am I?
I heard clapping upon the sky.

Sajed, a 19-year-old from Iraq, had come with his two sisters, Dina and Triza. Sajed was always at English classes; he was keen to master the English language. He wrote a number of articles and the following is an uncensored version of one of them:

> An Iraqi once mixed up 'kitchen' with 'chicken'. At the supermarket in London he wanted a piece of chicken and asked for a 'kitchen'. He was shown to a third floor that sold the kitchens.
>
> 'But I want a kitchen,' he said. Then he made the sound of a hen and flapped his arms like the wings of a chicken and pretended to sit on an egg.
>
> The staff began to laugh. They knew what he wanted now. It was a good lesson and the person never made the same mistake again.

The flaw in the above article was that it contained the word 'Iraqi'. It had passed ACM, DIMIA and the interpreters but someone spotted it after the newsletters were distributed. Fearing some kind of Iraqi vendetta, two staff members rushed out into the main compound to retrieve as many of the newsletters as they could. Several hundred newsletters were then run off without the offending word. The Iraqis just laughed and one said, 'We didn't take any offence—how could we? An Iraqi told the story.'

Among the Iraqis were Thamer, Amin and Kazim. Thamer and Amin were both qualified in information technology and were keen to start life anew in Australia, having, they said, been persecuted as Shiites after the Gulf War. Having come from Iraq, they stood a good chance of gaining a temporary visa, but Thamer would have to grind it out for eight months while Amin would be released after five months.

Kazim, an Iraqi, spoke English well and volunteered to translate the English version of the newsletter into Arabic. Kazim had graduated in Baghdad as a veterinary surgeon but, he said, had fled southern Iraq after his friends were tortured for worshipping as Shiites. His father, who had been detained because of his religious beliefs, had persuaded Kazim to leave Iraq.

After two weeks' suspension, Jalil was cleared of hitting a child in the computer centre incident. He took charge of the library with his wife and two teenage daughters helping out. With a simplified lending system that we had organised, he kept track of all the books and magazines, many of the recent ones having been donated by charitable organisations. Most of the material was in English; however, we ordered a number of Farsi and Arabic books, along with their respective dictionaries. A friend of Jalil's, Morteza, was often in the library. He was a quiet, studious person from Iran, a veterinarian.

During a few spare moments Jalil would talk about his application which had been rejected by the case officer. He was 43 years old and had been a literature teacher in Iran since 1979. His story was that while teaching at a primary school some security officers had arrested him. He was interrogated harshly for two weeks about his alleged political statements against the Iranian Government in the classroom. In late 2000 Jalil made comments in an intermediate school about the dictatorship and corruption in Iran. The security officers came with a warrant for his arrest but Jalil managed to escape by going through the maintenance gate. From the school-yard, Jalil fled to his sister's house, as he was too afraid to go home. The following day, Jalil arranged tickets for himself and his family and they flew to Teheran. Once there, he found a smuggler who organised false passports. From Teheran, the smugglers arranged his route to Australia.

The case officer apparently did not believe, however, that Jalil would be of significant interest to the Iranian authorities. Jalil was not a member of a political group and in general was not regarded as a strong political activist. As a result, Jalil's fear of persecution in Iran, according to the case officer, was not well-founded. There was no other option for Jalil but to appeal to the Refugee Review Tribunal; he could not countenance the thought of returning home.

Specially assigned security officers looked after the unaccompanied minors. Most of them were teenage boys, aged 13 to 17. As

teachers, we had to fill out daily forms for their classroom attendance. Some came faithfully every day; others would rarely come.
Security officers would try to coax them into coming to school but
there were excuses, such as a late night playing cards or they were
feeling too depressed. A few spoke English quite well and we
encouraged them to help out with teaching the young children.
Ali, a bright lad from Afghanistan, seemed very keen to take on a
small teaching load with the 5–7 year olds. When his case was
rejected he felt he could no longer continue. In the same way
Mehdi, a 17-year-old, also from Afghanistan, helped out a lot as
an assistant teacher but became too despondent when his case was
also rejected.

Initially the numbers of unaccompanied minors hovered around
20 but towards the middle of the year there were over 60. It was
hard to imagine how some of them would cope with so little
English when released. In South Australia the Department of
Human Services was involved in placing them into foster homes.

One of the unaccompanied minors who did come to classes
faithfully every day was Anwar Ali, a 17-year-old from Afghanistan.
Anwar Ali said that he had four brothers and one sister. The
Taliban had beaten one of his brothers for not having a beard. The
Taliban also had taken his uncle while he was at a market. Later,
his father retrieved his body from someone's land. Anwar Ali said
he had left because of the cruelty of the Taliban and because they
especially targeted Hazaras and Shiite Muslims. In October 2000,
10 Taliban came to their village looking for young men to take to
the front line. They demanded that his brother be sent with them.
His father resisted and was severely beaten. Anwar Ali's brother
rushed to his father's aid and the Taliban shot his brother through
the heart, killing him instantly. After that, his father decided that
Anwar Ali must be the one to escape from Afghanistan. Another
uncle arranged for a person to accompany him to Indonesia. He
said goodbye to his companion as he boarded a small, overcrowded
boat, thinking he would not survive the journey at sea.

Anwar Ali picked up English through his efforts to learn: he was always willing to help out in any way.

It was a sad day to hear that Anwar Ali's claim for refugee status had been rejected by his case officer and that he then had to appeal to the RRT. Later, his emotional state caused the psychologist a lot of concern.

Another unaccompanied minor, Essa, was a 17-year old Hazara who said he was from Ghazni province in Afghanistan. In the classroom he showed a keenness to learn English. With a similar story to Anwar Ali, his family had suffered at the hands of the Taliban. The Taliban had come to their home and demanded money and weapons. They had no weapons. The Taliban had taken Essa's elder brother and killed him. After that, Essa's family decided that at least one person must survive so they sold a Jeep and some land and paid a smuggler for him to leave Afghanistan. A Pushtun smuggler, who spoke a little Hazaragi, lived nearby; he was the first link in the smuggling chain. Essa flew from Lahore in Pakistan to Jakarta. After spending 20 days in Indonesia, he boarded one of the six buses that headed for the coast. The Indonesian police stopped the buses but after an agreed sum was allegedly paid they moved off again for their boat rendezvous.

Essa arrived at the Woomera detention centre in December 2000 and was released five months later. While in the centre he felt as though he had been in prison. Having no freedom was the worst thing for him. Once, with an upset bowel and diarrhoea, he had had to wait a week for medical attention.

There were 14 other unaccompanied minors with Essa in the donga and most of the time they were bored.

'We were always asking,' Essa said, 'give us games or give us tapes. We had to be in our donga by 9.30 pm. We couldn't go out after that, but we wanted to see our elders. Then they changed the time to 11.30 pm and it was a little better.'

Two other unaccompanied minors who came regularly to classes despite having no progress in their cases were Imran, a bright-eyed 17-year-old, and Mahmood, a 12-year-old, who was always willing to help in any way, such as cleaning out the class-rooms. While many of the other unaccompanied minors gave up their class work in despair after six months of detention both Imran and Mahmood persisted, to their credit.

We continued the Friday-morning sessions with the detainee teachers to give them moral support. They aired their troubles and we had something arranged specially for them, such as a com-puter session or watching a video on some aspect of Australian life. Occasionally, the ACM-appointed interpreters helped to explain the importance of the child-protection document.

On one occasion, Shaheen, a Farsi interpreter, thought it would be a good idea to talk to them also about cultural differences. So he spoke openly about these. Some of the differences were: 'No' in Australia means 'no'. A 'no' is often polite in Iran if you are offered a cup of tea. But in Australia 'no' is a 'no'. There is not so much swearing in Australia (hard to believe). We shower every day. Smiling does not mean we are making advances. Staring is not done here. A 'sly' look is okay. Blowing your nose is all right and is better than lots of sniffing. We shout less here. We form queues when waiting to be served. You should know the boundaries; for example, teachers cannot help with visas. Bargaining is less or not at all.

The cost to convert the old defence and space facility into a detention centre was $25 million, courtesy of the taxpayer. Two new compounds, named Mike and November, were ready to receive new arrivals by the end of March. Each compound would house approximately 350 detainees. Each of the portable buildings or dongas would house about 20 people. Without doors to the separate compartments there would be no privacy. There would be a television and a video inside each donga and there would be air-conditioning and a fridge. As part of Phase Two, the capacity would increase so the centre would be able to accommodate around 2000 detainees.

November Compound

Photograph obtained from the Human Rights and Equal Opportunity
Commission's National Inquiry into Children in Immigration Detention:
reproduced from website http://www.humanrights.gov.au/index.html

When we arrived on 29 March, Ellen, the support services
manager, requested we spend $50,000 on teaching resources for the
two new compounds by the end of the day. Peter and I had to
cancel school and delve into heaps of school catalogues and put
together a wish list. Never had we spent so much in so little time.
A highlight of the next day, though, was a visit by Gillian
Rubenstein, authoress, storyteller and a dual winner of the
Children's Book of the Year Award. She entertained the children
with selected readings from her books and then left a collection for
the library.

In April, the mood of the centre took a dive, with a number of
people, especially Iranians, being refused visas. Particularly distressing was a Baha'i family from Iran. The father, Siavash, was an
engineer and had shown his adaptability by taking charge of the

sewing room. His daughters, Sarah and Sahar, and eight other detainees assisted him. His wife, Falkanaz, helped as an assistant in the library. Mohammed, their 10-year-old son, was a bright lad but did not fit in with the other children. He fought more than once with some of his classmates. As their cases dragged on, Falkanaz, usually so radiant, became more despondent. Once, she broke down in the library sobbing uncontrollably. We tried to comfort her as best we could.

Of the many coming out of Iran the Baha'is seemed to have been genuinely persecuted. The prophet-founder of the Baha'i faith is Baha'Ullah, who was born in Iran. The Baha'is regard him as the most recent in a line of messengers from God who included Moses, Krishna, Buddha, Christ and Mohammed. Baha'is recognise the divine origin of all major religions. A central theme of the Baha'i faith is the oneness of humanity. Unfortunately, Islamic fundamentalists regard Baha'is as heretics and approximately 300,000 of them in Iran are denied legal or civil rights. The persecution intensified following the Islamic revolution in Iran in 1979 with many losing their properties and possessions as well as suffering arbitrary detention, torture and even execution.

Mehrdad, our Farsi interpreter, confirmed that because the Afghanis were at war and living under a more oppressive regime, they were more likely to obtain a visa than Iranians. Conditions in Iran were better now compared to 10 or 20 years earlier under the strict fundamentalist regime of Khomeni. However, Jalil, our librarian, said that there was not so much difference now and that President Khatami played second string to the fundamentalist religious leader, Ayatollah Khamenei, who was supported by the Soldiers of the Party of God. President Khatami and his allies in government had so far shown themselves unable to control the hard line elements that showed their allegiance to the earlier leaders of the Islamic Revolution. Shortly after President Khatami's re-election, Iran's conservative judiciary sentenced a militant supporter of Mr Khatami's reform program, Ms Haqiqqatjoo, to

22 months in prison on a number of charges, including propaganda against the regime.

Despite the apparent harshness of its regime, Iran was at the same time one of the most generous hosts in the world for refugees, sheltering around two million Afghanis and Iraqis with very little outside help.

Whatever the truth, according to the Australian Government, Australia's relationship with Iran had improved. The Iranian asylum seekers, therefore, had to have a watertight case otherwise they would be refused a TPV. Although people were not accepted as refugees because of their settlement potential, the Iranians with their professional and trade skills would probably do better in Australia than the Afghanis, many of whom were illiterate. Another reason for tension building up, according to Mehrdad, was that many of the Afghanis had been living in Iran or Pakistan and could have continued living there without threat. This had caused problems with the Iranians as well as those Afghanis fleeing Afghanistan who regarded themselves as genuine candidates for claiming refugee status. Among themselves, the Afghanis knew who had been living in Pakistan. Despite the interviewers bringing in linguistic experts and asking local-knowledge questions, most of the Pakistani-living Afghanis who had prepared themselves well had managed to obtain their visas, much to the chagrin of others who considered their own cases to be the true ones.

One day we arrived at the Golf Three gate to watch an Iranian being wristlocked by two security officers and walked out of the main compound. They said he had lost his temper and started to assault people with chairs on hearing that only Afghanis were being released.

Haman, our assistant Iranian teacher, became depressed about this time and said, 'I don't know what will become of me.'

There is a special grieving day, Ashoora, for the Shiite leader, Hussein. A follower of Mohammed and one of his heirs, he had fallen into disfavour with the Sunni Muslims. Hussein became a martyr and a saint after he and some 70 others were killed in battle in the 7th century. On this day many Shiite people wear black and some use chains to beat themselves. So on 5 April about 200 men and boys walked around the main compound of the Woomera centre chanting and striking themselves on the chest. The security officers kept a close watch.

There were also some light-hearted events. One of these was the Iranian New Year—celebrated with a concert in which both Afghanis and Iranians sang and danced. One of the Iranian singers had real talent and had everyone clapping. Later, we celebrated further in one of the classrooms with sweets, cakes and Coke. A couple of men dressed up as clowns and entertained us.

Pam and Sharon, the recreational officers, had arranged a sports day for young and old for the next day. It was a huge success with most people supporting the event. The three-legged race provided some hilarious moments. Some of the contestants, though, fell and scraped their skin on the rough stony surface. Mehrdad, the interpreter, fell heavily and had to be patched up at the medical centre.

Not to be outdone, the detainees in Sierra compound held an evening party—volleyball followed by a barbecue. Peter, the manager, and I joined in as volleyball recruits, playing for an hour. Afterwards, the detainees were perfect hosts as we all relaxed in the balmy night air—mesmerised by Arabic music and the swaying movement of dancers.

Any semblance of teaching order, though, was lost with a sudden influx of Iraqis into the main compound. Peter had more than 30 women in his class, some with babies. It was to be the start of a new musical compound game with those who had their third interview being put into the main compound. Others would be screened out after their first interview into the new compound, named November, or ultimately Sierra compound, renamed Oscar. Those coming in off the boats would be put into India compound or the other new compound, Mike, awaiting their interviews. Those who fought or caused trouble would be shifted into Oscar.

Teaching became a nightmare with these new movements. Often there was disruption with too many children or adults coming into the classrooms. Children especially liked to form working friendships and settle into a pattern of activities in a classroom. All that went by the board.

Two families of Kurds from north-eastern Iraq (Iraqi Kurdistan), also came into the main compound. Dilsad and his wife approached me with their son, Rabar, a 10-year-old, and two younger daughters, Dedir and Lava. The children seemed keen to go to school so we fitted them in as best we could.

Salem and I sorted the Iraqi men out into a beginners' and an advanced group. There were about 25 in each class and they were eager to learn. For a few weeks the teaching went well and the Iraqis seemed to enjoy the classes. Then a new wave of Afghani boat people arrived and suddenly we had 40 to 50 in one classroom.

The Iraqis took exception to this invasion and most decided to leave. Without any spare classrooms or spare teachers—even if we had wanted to—it was not possible to cater for each nationality on a separate basis. Later on, I took on Afghani assistant teachers who spoke English quite well and who were able to look after all the Afghani beginners.

Everyone seemed to be overworked and stressed out with the new arrivals. The Iraqis were in good spirits but already there were minor tiffs between them and the other detainees. Even in the computer room there were some arguments and one Iraqi came to me and said, 'We need an Arabic computer teacher, not one who speaks Farsi.' We tried to accommodate that, with Zeyad giving classes in Arabic. The six computers were fully used from morning till dusk with demand far exceeding supply. We tried to roster all the different groups—men, women and children, Afghanis, Iraqis and Iranians, with two to a computer—and not cause a diplomatic incident. The typing programs, Phonics Alive, and Typequick, were very popular. The programs for English, drawing and desktop publishing were also used a lot: Alphabet, Interactive Picture

Dictionary, Paint, Corel Draw and Adobe Photoshop. And some were tackling Microsoft Word to type letters and résumés.

The computer craze continued. Pam once took the young boys for sporting activities and mentioned the word 'computer'. With that cue all the boys ran to the computer centre and lined up. We had to explain to them that we would allow them in later. On another occasion I passed the boys playing a kind of cricket in the compound but when they saw me they stopped playing and raced towards the computer centre.

In the last week of April, Trish gave warnings at a staff meeting, passed on by an ACM intelligence officer, that the mood of the detainees had deteriorated. Detainees who had been sent back to Woomera from Port Hedland had set the mess alight during the night. Also, women were sewing up their lips as a form of protest. There could be another flare-up. We were to be on guard and report anything, no matter how small. If we were feeling uncomfortable in any way we were to come out of the compound. We did not get paid to get hurt. The sole security officer at Golf Three gate did not give us any comfort either. 'I've seen it all—the riots at Curtin and Woomera—been bashed, threatened and kicked. If anything happens I'll be out of here. You can fend for yourselves,' he said.

The next day a group of detainees gathered at the Golf Three gate of the main compound, protesting at the lack of progress in the processing of their cases. Eventually, they dispersed. Haman came to me sobbing, saying that he was too upset and could no longer teach English. Amir did not turn up at the computer centre and when I met him his ashen face and poor demeanour was a reflection of his state. As part of a general hunger strike, he had not eaten for two days. It was becoming a common occurrence—many were complaining that after three months they had had only one interview while others had had their second and third interviews with their migration agents and case officers.

While the hunger strike was on, many were turning up at the medical centre with various complaints. Bernice, the doctor, told me how on a previous strike they had been taken to the local Woomera hospital and put on intravenous drips. Some had had to be restrained to prevent them interfering with the drip. They had recovered and fortunately did not go on another hunger strike.

Bernice also described how stressful it was working in the medical centre—12-hour shifts, so many cases, always a backlog and working in a confined space. On top of that they had their own interpersonal conflicts. She felt strongly about the people in Oscar—many had not even got to their second interview after three or more months. 'They should be told that they have been refused a visa. It's unfair to them,' she said. 'Now, after eighteen months some detainees are still waiting for the results of the Refugee Review Tribunal and the Federal Court.'

Some of the Iranians and Iraqis started looking for private lawyers. It would cost them $1500 or more and this was prohibitive for most. Jalil and Salem, our two assistants, and another Iraqi, Adnan, contacted Dr Mohamed Al Jabiri, a human rights support and migration consultant. Dr Jabiri had worked with the United Nations for many years and had an intimate knowledge of the Iraqi regime and he knew Saddam Hussein well.

Adnan spoke English quite well and always greeted me cheerfully in the compound. He said his problems had started when his father had been dismissed from his job as a high-ranking public servant when he'd opposed Saddam Hussein's Baa'th Party. His brother had protested against the Government's action and been imprisoned; he had managed to escape from prison after the Gulf War and flee to Turkey. Because of this, Adnan had been arrested and tortured over his brother's activities. Adnan was released after two weeks, but the authorities had continued to hound him. He had then decided to leave Iraq.

There were some brighter moments at this uncertain time though—two of the teenage girls, Shaima and Tayabba, were released. Because it all happened so quickly there was not a chance to say goodbye. Not having this opportunity grieved us as we knew there was little likelihood of seeing them again. Both were strong-spirited girls and, although complaining about their visa situation, had never become despondent. Now, Hafizah, a friend of both girls, came to me and cried, 'I'm the only girl left now from my boat. What will become of me?' I tried to console her and said to try to be patient. Hafizah was mature beyond her teenage years—she had grown up fast in Afghanistan and had discovered a measure of compassion and strength within herself. Although troubled by events in the past, she refused quietly to succumb to them and was not embittered.

With Haman having a rest from teaching English, some Afghanis asked me if I could take on the beginners' class. With some reshuffling of the timetable I started teaching them. Four turned up for the first class. I got to know them quite well over the next few days. Then the numbers started to increase and before I knew it we had more than 20.

Several were illiterate and said they had come from a simple, farming background and lived in a small village. One of them was a 23-year-old Pushtun, Tawab. His family had observed the Shiite Muslim religion that had put them in disfavour with the Taliban. Three years earlier the Taliban had come to his family home searching for weapons; they had not found any. Instead, they had taken his elder brother. Later the Taliban had informed the family that he had been killed in the front line. His father feared that the same fate would befall Tawab and arranged for him to leave Afghanistan.

Arif had a similar story. He was a 22-year-old, born, he said, in Paktia province in Afghanistan. He too was a Pushtun and worshipped as a Shiite Muslim. The Taliban had taken one of his brothers and two other men from the village and, after three years, there had been no word from them. His father had worked as a farmer and thought it would be better if Arif left Afghanistan. Arrangements were made for Arif to cross into Pakistan with a smuggler, and then to fly to Indonesia.

Tawab introduced me to another Pushtun, Ghulam, who told me he had been living in a refugee camp in Pakistan, close to the border with Afghanistan, since his family had fled the civil war 12 years earlier. At first they had lived in a tent and later they had been able to build a house out of mud bricks. The Taliban had taken their father from the refugee camp one and a half years earlier and there had been no word of him. Ghulam had been scared of being taken by the Taliban, so with the money from the sale of their house, he had paid a smuggler who had taken him to Lahore and then to Indonesia. Ghulam would find it difficult to return to Pakistan without formal documents and, if he were sent back to the camp, he felt he would still be in danger from the Taliban.

Being a Pushtun and a Sunni should have been enough protection against the Taliban but there were other factors. For instance, Abbas told me he was a 31-year-old Pushtun and a Sunni from Afghanistan; he had worked in a laboratory as a malarial technician. One of his elder brothers had worked in Kabul for the Rabbani regime and been killed by rocket fire when the Taliban took over the city in 1996. He and his brother had been members of the Jamiat-e-Islami Party led by President Rabbani. As was the custom with Pushtuns, there was a code of vengeance where any wrong done to you or your family must be avenged in the course of time to even the score. In this case, one year after Abbas's brother was killed, distant relatives who were vindictive against Abbas's family had sought vengeance by reporting that Abbas's brother had died in a shoot-out with the Taliban. Abbas, fearing the Taliban's retribution on himself, fled to Jalalabad with his wife and children and continued his work there as a technician in a laboratory. After four years another, older, brother was arrested by the Taliban and Abbas had new fears of being arrested himself so in April 2001 he had left Pakistan for Australia.

Sarah Lumley joined us as a new teacher on 1 May. Now we were three. She was particularly keen to help out with the 'littlies' as she described the 5–7s and kindy children. We desperately needed someone who could look after the youngsters. Neither Peter nor I really fitted the bill but Sarah, with her experience in teaching junior school children, was ideal.

Shortly after, Sarah wrote an account of her encounters for the *Gibber Gabber*, the Woomera community newspaper:

Controversial, daunting, open to question—why would a primary school teacher from a big city want to move to the South Australian desert to work in a detention centre for illegal immigrants? Friends in Sydney were surprised, raised an eyebrow as to why I would want to help people who had come in 'through the back door'. Above all, they were curious.

I arrived at the double gates rather alarmed at the security measures. Kitted out in a navy uniform and equipped with a radio, I couldn't see how I could relate this to sitting on a carpet reading a story about a princess to five-year-olds. Every teacher has first-day nerves with a new class, but these pupils could barely speak a word of English and were from a different culture. How could I manage?

A little girl comes breezing into my classroom, red anorak zipped up, hood string gathered around her face to protect her from the wind. 'Hello Missy. Class?'

'Yes, class,' I reply, astonished at her vibrancy. Weren't these children supposed to be unhappy most of the time having been through traumatic experiences? But children are remarkably resilient. This is not to say they have not suffered, have not been traumatised and have not witnessed atrocities. Any child that is crammed on to a boat carrying many times its capacity would be traumatised. And yes, this does have an impact. But living in the here and now, as children do for a lot of the time, they are prey to all the normal emotions—playfulness, curiosity, mischief, boredom. So the children that raced through my room that day with canvas school bags on their backs were like any other children I've ever taught. They settled on to the mat, shuffled, elbowed their too-close neighbour out of the way and then tuned into my foreign voice.

They later painted pictures of square houses with triangle roofs, chimneys, smoke, flowers in the garden and a big sunshine in the sky. Just like the children all over Australia. And they weren't different or diseased or running ragged around the accommodation area. In fact, many possess an enthusiasm for school that I've rarely encountered. At the end of the class they groaned, used every delaying tactic possible to stay in the classroom, and hung around the door.

I realised, as I put the paintings on the wall, that for these children I am the face of Australia. And what I do with them not only prepares them for their impending experiences in the wider community but will set their models of expectation and reaction. For them, Woomera is Australia and I for one would like to project a positive image of Australia as their first impression.

A few weeks on, I am not daunted by the double gates, the centre does not have a feeling of a prison at all, and most importantly I don't feel that these children are not deserving of my time as they are 'illegal'. Once my classroom door closes at 9 am, it is like any other classroom in Australia. I think about my lessons for the week, what resources to prepare, and wonder how many new faces I will see, and how many I will say goodbye to.

(31 May 2001, *Gibber Gabber*)

On the same day as Sarah's arrival, a number of Iraqis were put into Oscar; some of them had been fighting; others said they were onlookers, or just caught up in the melee. Then it was alleged that one of them had upset a glass of water in the mess and would not clean it up when requested by an Iranian. Fighting broke out again and two were injured. One was sent to the hospital with a suspected arm fracture. We were not allowed into Oscar, so instead I concentrated some effort on November compound where about 300 new arrivals, mostly Afghanis, had been placed. Many were keen to start English classes.

One of the newcomers to November compound was a 29-year-old Iranian, Mehrzad. He was a very friendly person, spoke English well and was keen to assist in the teaching program. I said he could start classes as soon as the medical staff, who had been using the educational centre as a temporary clinic, had moved out. Mehrzad turned out to be a great asset, teaching two or more classes a day with about 30 attending each class.

Later Mehrzad talked about his background. He had been brought up in a devout Muslim family but he himself had never really believed in Islam. Instead, he had become a Christian after having contact with Christians. He now feared persecution if he returned to Iran because of his new faith. I could well imagine that he would not receive a favourable response from the case officer reviewing his application for refugee status. Other Iranians who were now in Oscar had also converted to Christianity and were not granted visas. There were two reasons: firstly, although disadvantaged, it was considered that they would not be unduly persecuted if they returned to Iran, and secondly, they might have concocted their story of conversion to Christianity to make a plausible case for a visa. In the coming weeks I would realise that Mehrzad was a deep-thinking and sincere person and that he had not changed his faith lightly.

In the main compound, two women who had previously taught in Iraq, Entesar and Emam, wanted to help with the 8–12s class. That was great, so I provided the material and they worked well together. This allowed me to start a class with about 25 children of the same age group in November compound. Ali Reza, a 25-year-old Iranian, was only too happy to help as an assistant, so while Mehrzad taught the adults in the educational centre we taught the children in the mess after the breakfast clean-up.

As usual, I tried to learn their names first and this helped to establish a rapport with the children. There were names I had never heard of before, such as Manoochr, Emad, Adil, Murtada, Azita, Mandana, Batul and Sapideh.

One of the mothers, Cobra, brought in her six-year-old son, Sohrab. I explained that it was really a class for 8–12-year-olds. She insisted, saying her son was bright and could already speak some English. We agreed to give him a try.

Cobra apparently had had an upsetting time in her six-year-old marriage. Over many disagreements her husband had become violent and hit her. A divorce had been arranged with Sohrab coming under his father's care. Cobra had tried to leave Iran legally, for England, to work as a nurse. Her husband had become angry and jealous when another man appeared on the scene. He had threatened to kill her and Sohrab if she did not remarry him. For Sohrab's sake she had agreed. After the marriage it had been worse than before. The next time she had left with Sohrab and without her husband's permission.

The children all worked away with an animated buzz enjoying a whole host of simple language-learning activities and basic mathematics. They were in for the long haul because many of the children's parents had been screened out in November compound. While the parents anguished over their future the children seemed more resilient. They were a lively lot, participating in classroom activities as well as those arranged for them by the recreational officer. In the longer term, however, even the children would suffer because of their parents' distress.

Ali Reza was an aspiring teacher, and had hopes of continuing his chosen profession in Australia. He said the Government of Iran had targeted him because of his involvement in student demonstrations at Teheran University. He had fled to Australia to escape imprisonment and torture.

He provided excellent assistance with the teaching and we were able to make progress in the children's ability to speak, write and read English. Fortunately, we did this without the usual shifting and disruption of classes by DIMIA's policy of movement of detainees to other compounds with the stages of processing. Ali Reza would often have to look after the children until I arrived a few minutes late from the main compound. When I entered the mess the children would burst into a deafening cheer. Then we settled down and started our English hour followed by mathematics. Two Iranians, Mosen and Mouiad, also came in to help us. They could not speak much English but were keen to teach.

Although there was an educational centre comprising a classroom for 30 adults and a computer centre allocated to both Mike and November compounds, there were no chairs, tables or whiteboards. Despite this, we decided to launch out and either use the mess or have the detainees take chairs from the mess to the classrooms. With the recent arrival of detainees there was a spurt of initial enthusiasm for learning English. The Arabic and Farsi interpreters joined in and we coped with large classes of more than 50 at a time. As we co-opted more detainees to assist and run some of the classes, we reduced the class number of each to a more manageable group of 25 to 30. On our roll book we had over 30 assistants and we were running about 25 one-hour classes a day.

One of the problems that the detainees faced was boredom. English classes provided only one or two hours at most for adults. Even for children it was difficult to slot in more than two hours of contact time. So the recreational and social welfare officers devised a whole range of activities, such as women's meetings, children's club after school, art and craft, board and card games, sewing, special sports events, mural painting and Aussie dingo. Aussie dingo was a huge success and run like Aussie bingo which was a gambling game—we could not have that without raising questions.

There were specific centres for women, men and the unaccompanied minors, where they could meet or take part in some of the indoor recreational activities, such as table tennis. A music centre was opened in the main compound and one of the Afghanis, Hakim, an accomplished musician, ran classes for men and children. I would send some of the children up to Hakim each day and he let them play on the keyboard, drums, percussion instruments, recorders and guitars. Bijan meanwhile continued with his meditation classes and I provided him with another selection of relaxing music cassettes.

Everyone was in danger of being mobbed if they handed out 'freebies'. On one occasion, Irene, the social welfare officer, with Peter assisting, handed out wool to the women. Queuing and orderly behaviour were out as Peter and Irene were hemmed in from all sides, with outstretched arms eager to grasp the wool lots. On another occasion, Sharon tried to systematise the delivery of wool, taking the names of women requesting wool. The number pressing in on her grew to about 40. She was pushed against a wall and felt quite vulnerable so she left without distributing the wool.

Special events included an occasional concert, children's parties and barbecues. A local police officer often came to the centre to talk on matters such as obtaining legal advice and driving in Australia.

The local Catholic priest, Father Jim, and Sister Anne visited the centre regularly to help those of the Christian faith and anyone else who was interested. The Sabian Mandeans had only one visit from a religious leader, a sheikh from Sydney; they were on their own so they welcomed Father Jim to their services. The Christians and Sabian Mandeans worshipped together on some occasions and apart on others. There were separate holy or feast days for Christians and Sabian Mandeans and they invited Sister Anne to attend these. Mass was celebrated weekly in the separate compounds. On the one occasion an imam from Adelaide visited the centre there was a demonstration by some frightened detainees. Sister Anne tried to calm them down saying that the imam was there to bring peace and harmony. With little outside support the Muslim detainees organised their own prayer and other religious services.

Father Jim suggested using St Michael's Primary School in the Woomera township as it was no longer used for teaching. ACM, however, declined as it would tie up buses and security staff.

A new psychologist, Darryl, arrived in the second week of May and he voiced a concern about some of the children not coming to school and those with obvious behavioural problems. Along with Marie and Harold, the other psychologists, they did their best to help. With so many referrals and no office space, though, it was difficult to make headway with any of the problems facing children or adults. A 'patch up' job was the best they could hope for. There were deep underlying causes of dysfunctional behaviour, not surprising considering their traumatic past and even the present within the Woomera centre environment.

Shortly after, I shook hands with Kolam, our 8-year-old 'terror' with a file so thick it would have impressed a criminal with a 20-year record. I wished him and his brother, Azim, all the best. They were nonplussed as they stood outside the property office awaiting their bus to take them to Sydney. With them was Amin, an Iraqi who had attended the advanced English classes. He was overjoyed but his joy was short-lived as DIMIA realised they had made a mistake. Someone else with a similar name was the lucky one. Amin was a sorry sight as he trudged back into the main compound with his suitcase.

Also released at this time were a six-year-old boy and a 13-year-old girl. Both had been hyperactive and had caused much disruption in classes. I heaved a sigh of relief, not just from a teacher's point of view, but I hoped they might receive the kind of support they needed.

Too many men were coming to the English classes. We could cope with only about 25 in each of the classrooms but sometimes there was standing room only. I managed to obtain half a donga for another class and that was it. No more room was allowed. We started hiring more detainee teachers, both men and women, to run classes in the afternoon as well as the evening in the main compound. It was not sufficient—we had run out of classrooms during the day and the children suffered in contact time with only two or three morning sessions while we taught mainly adults in the afternoon and evening. We needed more classrooms and more Australian teachers to cope with all five compounds. Fortunately, in Mike compound, two Iraqi women, Parvin and Regina, both teachers by profession, were able to take the children. Parvin was part of a small group of Sabian Mandeans who had just arrived; they revered John the Baptist. Both Parvin and Regina were excellent teachers and, with little supervision, taught the children English.

On 17 May, the Baha'i family, Siavash, his wife, Falkanaz, and their three children, Sahar, Sarah and Mohammed, were released. They were overjoyed when they heard the good news and we breathed a sigh of relief to know that they had finally won their cases for temporary visas. It was good to know also that there was some hope for the Iranians. The picture looked bleak elsewhere though. Most of the Iranians were screened out after only one interview and sent to the November compound. For myself, going into November was like meeting the condemned. The security officers made comments such as 'they haven't any hope' and 'they'll be sent back'. They looked a subdued lot with the sword of Damocles hanging over them.

Inese, our new teacher, arrived to replace Peter. The farewell for Peter was overwhelming. His teenage girls sang, shouted and yodelled—it was all too much. The noise was heard from one end of the main compound to the other. Then all the cards and tributes followed. Poor Inese—it was a hard act to follow. Peter recounted some of his happy moments with them, including how he was bowled over in the wool handing-out episode. 'Gimme yellow, gimme red, gimme blue,' he called out re-enacting the scene. The teenage boys were sad too, although they did not display the same degree of emotion.

I had really valued Peter's qualities and his friendship. Peter had just missed out seeing Hafizah, one of the remaining girls, who had been in his class from the start, being released with her three younger brothers and two sisters. Although I did not manage to say goodbye, she left a drawing by Sadiq, the artist, with a thank-you note on the back.

By the end of May we were up to 939 detainees (Iraqi 29.5 per cent; Iranian 17.4 per cent; Afghan 51.3 per cent) with the numbers in each compound being: Main 414; November 315; Mike 178; and Oscar 32). The number of unaccompanied minors was now 47 and the number of children overall was 218 (23.2 per cent).

The Opposition's Immigration Spokesman, Con Sciacca, spent the day in Woomera on 30 May 2001. He visited the children and commented: 'I must say that if there is anything that I took away that really stuck with me, it is the faces of little children in these detention centres.

'Now, again, may I say that they are not being maltreated. Quite the contrary. They were being given school lessons and they were trying to learn English . . . To me it's tragic to see little children, as young as well, in prams, in that sort of environment,' he said.

On being asked by the interviewer: 'Con, do you support mandatory detention for illegal immigrants?' He replied, 'Look, Labor in fact introduced mandatory detention. And so I have to be—I have to be absolutely clear on that. We introduced mandatory detention. We are not going to get rid of mandatory detention in the sense that we don't believe that if you come in here unauthorised that you should be without papers, without documents, without us knowing who you are . . . that you need to be checked first before you could be let out into the community.'

On the last day of May I started the day at 6.30 am when it was still dark and no-one was making demands such as, 'I want the daily averages of adults and children attending classes urgently', or 'Have you done the monthly report?'

The English class with the 8–12s in the main compound was first and Eman helped out. Then, after opening up and checking the computer centre, the library and the kindergarten, I raced over to November compound to take the 8–12s again, with Ali Reza's assistance. After, I had an hour on simple conversational exercises with about 60 men in the educational centre. And then in the afternoon it was on to Mike compound but the game Aussie dingo was on and nothing could take its place. Still, 15 turned up for English classes instead of about 60 on the previous day. Then I took a brisk walk back to the main compound for an advanced English lesson. After finishing at 5 pm. there was a CERT (Centre Emergency Response Team) call and I could not leave the compound. One of the detainees in Oscar compound had climbed on to the roof of one of the buildings and threatened to throw himself off if he were not allowed to make a phone call. About an hour later he was granted his wish and I went home.

Most days after arriving home I would be emotionally drained, not from the teaching but from everything else. The clamouring of voices and disquiet of the centre were in complete contrast to the quiet, ghost-like town of Woomera. Liz, my wife, in contrast to myself, was completely relaxed and relished the change of pace in her life, not minding at all the almost surreal peacefulness of the town. At the end of the day I would force myself to jog a little into the bush surrounding the town. Often I would spot some kangaroos or emus or even a few sheep grazing on the saltbush. After, I would relax a little, but the voices of unrest were still there and I would wake up in the early hours of the morning and hear them again.

OVERLOAD AT WOOMERA
(1 June–4 September 2001)

Winter began with a warm sunny day and two emergencies. Shahin in November compound asked me to help write a letter to DIMIA requesting that they answer questions about the delays in processing. We discussed the situation and wrote a letter to the DIMIA head at Woomera, coming from Shahin as the representative of November compound:

'We have been here for two to three months and would like to ask some questions concerning the delay in our processing. We would appreciate meeting with you or your representative to discuss the situation.'

There had been talk about a demonstration but I suggested that the letter would be a better way. 'If there is no progress after a certain time you could think about a peaceful demonstration,' I advised.

Marie, the psychologist, described the horrors of a sea voyage for a young mother and her daughter. The ship had run out of fuel but luckily a coastguard had spotted them. They were safe, but now the mother had just received notice of her visa refusal. The woman had broken down. 'What can I do? Oh God! Oh God! Oh God!' she cried. Marie tried her best to help her.

I finished the monthly report in a flurry. Brian, our administrative officer, could not read my scrawl and had changed 'mathematics' into 'emetics'. I did not pick it up either in the typewritten version—at least not straightaway—so it went through to the higher echelons of ACM and DIMIA. Maybe it did not matter anyway.

With the extra people coming into the detention centre we were stretched to the limit. There were incessant demands coming from all quarters: from the administration section for daily statistics on attendance at classes, library and computer centre, attendance by unaccompanied minors, hours worked by assistant teachers; from the assistant teachers for teaching material and aids; from the detainees attending classes for pens, pencils, rubbers, exercise books, drawing paper, dictionaries and readers; and from detainees in general for books, cigarettes, writing and drawing material, dictionaries and assistance with their cases. The latter usually involved trying to explain simply some legal terms in a letter or document.

On 6 June I turned up to work at 6.30 am. A storm had raged all night. I arrived in a surreal setting of camp lights cascading their beams on pools of muddy water. A virtual quagmire greeted us everywhere; it was easy to spot the low-lying areas—one in front of a classroom. The boys had no qualms about wading through it and dragging red clay mud on their shoes into the classroom.

Then all the new arrivals from Mike compound overwhelmed us. Packed bodies filled each room. There were more than 50 unaccompanied minors in one room. Some of these were definitely over 20. How could they be classed as minors? We were in no position to argue with the authorities—their birthdays were recorded as being on 31 December or 1 January and nothing could change that now. Inese, who wanted to take charge of the education of all the unaccompanied minors, threw up her arms in despair. Parvin, our assistant in Mike, had also come over and taken charge of a packed class for the 8–12s. Eman had bowed out gracefully and Entesar and her son had been released so Parvin's help was most welcome.

In the afternoon we turned our attention to adults in the main compound. It was a complete shambles with scores of new people coming to classes. To the rescue came Jalil and Haman as well as two newcomers, Aref and Yadzan, from Afghanistan. All could speak reasonable English and so I gave them immediate teacher status.

We struggled through the next day with the fierce biting winds of winter upon us. In the afternoon three of the hired teachers did

Detainees in the main compound pushing on Golf Gate Two.
Note the double internal fence with a coil of razor wire in between.

not turn up for various reasons and we had two classrooms packed
with more than 40 men and another half-sized classroom with 20
awaiting their teachers. The women were also without a teacher.
After sending out an SOS two of the new teachers arrived, plus a
fill-in for the women.

Ominous clouds of a different kind, though, were brewing in our
midst. The first warning that something had gone awry was the
sight of bleary-eyed security officers the next day. Most had had
only an hour or two of sleep, if that. The detainees in the main
compound had started rioting at about 6 pm the previous evening.
The riot-geared officers had swung into action but could not
prevent the rampage that followed. The rioters trashed the mess,
breaking windows and two computers in the process. As well, they
broke into the music room and destroyed all the musical instruments. About eight hours later they dispersed and the security officers resumed control. The trouble had started when four Afghanis
who had not been granted their temporary protection visas decided
to vent their feelings of rage, with the help of other detainees.

At 10.30 am it all threatened to erupt again. The water tankers moved into position and security officers raced for their riot gear. The programs staff were ushered out for the Queen's Birthday long weekend. As we came into Woomera a war-sounding siren summoned the off-duty security officers back to the centre.

While the security staff attended to the quelling of the rioters and bringing order to the Woomera centre most of the programs staff enjoyed a brief respite, having the Queen's Birthday holiday on Monday as well as the Friday.

I drove back to Gawler and stopped on the way at Port Augusta and happened to meet Irene and Pam at a cafe in the main street. They were also having a pit stop on the way to Adelaide. We agonised with a sense of foreboding and sorrow over the maelstrom of despair that had engulfed the detention centre.

In Gawler I met the president of the Gawler Refugee Association, Pat Sheahan, to talk about the possibility of sponsoring from Pakistan, Sarwar, an Afghani who had already been rejected as an applicant for refugee status in Australia. The association had already helped to welcome and settle Vietnamese and Croatian families in Gawler.

There had been a lot of talk in the community about 'queue jumpers'—those who bypass the approved channels if they can. Sarwar, a friend of mine, was one of those who had tried to come to Australia through the appropriate channels. I had first met Sarwar in early 1980; he'd come to Roseworthy Agricultural College from Afghanistan to undertake a graduate diploma in agriculture. The course was sponsored by the Food and Agriculture Organisation (FAO) to provide training for agricultural personnel from the Near East, Middle East and North Africa in systems of dryland farming, as used in southern Australia.

Sarwar was a likeable character with a quiet, easy-going manner and a heart-warming smile. Behind his modest manner he was a proud Afghani believing that whatever he did in his education or profession would be for his country's benefit. He had been working at a government agricultural research station in Afghanistan. The

Russian army had just invaded Afghanistan to prop up the new communist regime.

After completing his diploma, Sarwar spoke to me about his dilemma. He could most likely remain in Australia if he were to seek refugee status or he could return to support his relatives who were now facing hardships under the communist regime. If he returned to Afghanistan he would have to take his chance that he would not be branded as a traitor for turning his eyes towards the West. It had been tempting to try and stay in Australia. An Afghani in the previous year's intake at Roseworthy had already gained refugee status. Sarwar made the big decision to go back to support his family members. Over the next few years we kept in touch— somehow most of the letters reached their destination despite the warring crises.

In 1981 Sarwar was arrested because he had an affiliation with the West. He was tortured while he was in jail for a year. On his release, he was fortunate to take up a position as manager of a horticultural research station near Kabul. This continued until 1992, when he was arrested by followers of the Hizbi-i-Wahdat Shia movement, which opposed the rapidly rising power group of the Taliban. He was transferred to Dasht-i-barchi, where he was tortured and his life threatened. Following a payment by his brother he was released after two months.

He fled to Pakistan. In 1994, about a year after his arrival in Pakistan, Sarwar became the provincial manager of Afghanaid, a British non-government organisation. In May 1995, while in Peshawar, Sarwar's eldest son, Ahmad, disappeared. Twenty-one months later he returned to Sarwar's home in Peshawar and told his story. While Ahmad had been at the supermarket a red vehicle had pulled up alongside and one of the passengers claimed he was a friend of his father and offered him a lift. As soon as he climbed into the vehicle he was knocked unconscious.

The abductors took Ahmad to an unknown family in a town in Afghanistan; someone said it was Kandahar. He worked in an

Beginners' class in English for men taken by an Afghan detainee as an assistant teacher

A class of mixed Afghani, Iraqi and Iranian children, aged 8–12

orchard, collected firewood and fetched water from a well. About a year later, a member of this family handed him over to another group. They trained him in the handling of weapons and told him that he would go and fight the infidels. As well, they tested him on lessons on the Koran and they beat him if he did not know the answers. Then Ahmad and others taken by the Taliban carried out assaults and raids on their enemies. Ahmad knew he would surely die fighting and resolved to escape. In February 1997 he feigned sickness and stayed in his room. He slipped out and made his way to Kabul, some 500 kilometres from Kandahar. From there, with the help of one of Sarwar's aunts, he was taken back to Peshawar. His three younger brothers were overjoyed at his return.

Because of the increase in fighting in early September 1997, and while Sarwar was managing Afghanaid's projects in Mazar-i-Sharif, all the staff had to escape by road to Peshawar. A local Afghanaid officer said later that Wahdat Party soldiers had been looking for Sarwar because they believed he had been spying for the Taliban. Sarwar, they said, used a satellite telephone to help direct artillery fire on Wahdat soldiers.

Then, in August 1998, the Taliban had, it was thought, again abducted Ahmad and there has been no word since. Sarwar also suffered other losses in his family during the reign of the Taliban. His uncle disappeared, the Wahdat Party killed two cousins and his father and brother both sustained serious injuries.

Sarwar then worked with the Norwegian Afghanistan Committee (NAC) from September 1999 as an officer in charge of the Ghazni and Kabul aid programs—various projects in education, health and engineering. Sarwar heard that the Taliban had arrested his brother in Kabul; he decided to go to Kabul to seek his release. The Taliban arrested Sarwar when he arrived.

The Taliban subjected Sarwar to a variety of tortures—whiplash, kneeling on gravel, electrical shock, strikes from a wooden baton and a hot ring placed over his wrist while they accused him of an affiliation with the West, and being against the

Taliban regime by supporting an opposition party. As a result, Sarwar had a burn mark on his wrist, lost two front teeth, had marks on his knees and back, and pain in his stomach and feet. Three months later, he escaped when his guards wandered off. He caught a bus to Torkham (Khyber Pass). The border was closed, so he crossed over to Pakistan by a smugglers' route.

Later, in Peshawar, two men entered his home and attacked him. They hit him in the eye, broke his nose and severely lacerated his index finger. He was taken to hospital where they had to amputate part of his finger. The police investigated the crime but could not find the culprits.

Sarwar submitted an application for migration to the Australian embassy in Islamabad under the refugee and humanitarian class in January 1997. Two years later the First Secretary of Immigration David Tanner, of the Australian High Commission Migration Office, advised Sarwar that the application was unsuccessful. He had not met the requirements for persecution in his home country.

In January 2001 the Taliban authorities in Ghazni informed the acting director of NAC that Sarwar was accused of siding with an opposition party. Because of these accusations and the potential risk to Sarwar and his family, NAC terminated his employment at the beginning of June 2001.

Sarwar had now achieved the unenviable distinction of being seen as a traitor by the Taliban, as a supporter of the West by communist remnants, and as a supporter of the Taliban by the Shiites. At that time, the Taliban operated across the border with impunity so there was no guarantee of safety in either Afghanistan or Pakistan. Sarwar's wife, Suraya, a graduate of the faculty of political science in Kabul University, had been housebound for six years and suffered from depression.

While working at Woomera detention centre I wrote to Sarwar asking him questions about those coming to Australia from Afghanistan. He replied that most of the Afghanis who used the smuggling routes had been living in Pakistan for one or two years.

A smuggler, Haji Ewaze, operated from Karachi; his price was US$6000 a person by boat. In Peshawar, another smuggler operated with the Jamal Travel Agency and the cost of the air and boat travel to Australia or New Zealand could vary from US$6000 to US$14,000.

Sarwar's story illustrates the difficulty of an apparently genuine claim being turned down. Irrespective of the merits of his case he faced more uncertainty and further delays if he proceeded down the 'right path' again. He had to provide the Australian High Commission with new evidence or he could take his case to the United Nations High Commissioner for Refugees (UNHCR) or he could wait until it was safe to return to Kabul. Or, out of desperation and if he had sufficient funds, he could take the smugglers' route to New Zealand, the preferred way after hearing about Australia's new policy of funding Pacific nations to process asylum seekers, 'the Pacific solution'.

On Tuesday 12 June, after the long weekend away from Woomera, we returned to pick up the pieces. The music room was completely vandalised—even the piano and keyboard were beyond repair. Hakim, our music teacher, was distraught—nothing would console him. The children's playroom had also been trashed. The puddles and mud everywhere cast a sombre veil over the whole scene. The display of weapons that I had first seen at the beginning of October last year had been brought out and photographed for the media.

Then I found out that there was no Amir at the computer centre or Aziz to take the children for sport or Bijan to help people relax. Along with four others, they had escaped. Aided by the soft ground they had used wire-cutters to break through the inner fence and dug their way out under the outer four-metre high, galvanised-iron palisade fence. Their chances of being released had to be considered slim, given the current climate against Iranians claiming refugee status. They had had nothing to lose.

Two days later 21 people were closely monitored by the high risk assessment team (HRAT) for fear of harming themselves. The team (the health services manager, the detention manager and the psychologist) presented documented evidence relevant to each detainee on a risk-treatment plan. Security officers then made observations on detainees at risk, the frequency of observations varying from two minutes (high risk) to two-hourly. The detainees were released from observations only after the team agreed that the detainee was no longer at risk.

There was drama in November compound next. Fortunately, and thanks in no small measure to Shahin, it was a peaceful protest. His previous letter had been passed to DIMIA with lots of signatures and there had been no response. They had sent a number of letters asking DIMIA to send someone to inform them of the progress of their applications. They decided to go on a hunger strike as a way of protesting peacefully.

After two days, they gathered near the front of the compound to protest more vigorously. The chanting of about 100 detainees outside the fence went on for over two hours: 'DIMIA, DIMIA, DIMIA'. Some raised their banners with messages: 'SOS', 'Freedom' and 'Visa'. The water cannon moved closer and Dave, the intelligence officer, recorded everything on video. It was peaceful, however. Shahin had said so. Finally, the DIMIA manager appeared, accompanied by the psychologist, medical officer, interpreters and security officers. The manager agreed to restart their claims if everyone said that they were seeking protection under the Refugee Convention. He sent some application forms for the detainees to fill in.

Jeremy Moore, a lawyer from Adelaide, had given Shahin the phrase, 'I am looking for protection and refugee status under the Refugee Convention'. This would permit the processing of applicants to continue. About a month later those who had filled in the forms had their second interview. Not everyone joined the protest or filled in the forms.

The intelligence officer was more pessimistic about any chances for them. He confided to me: 'Why do you think DIMIA have kept quiet? They've been screened out. If they tell them this there would be a riot, just like at Curtin. There's nowhere to go. They'll have to stay here until they decide to go back.'

The Sabian Mandeans believed there was no need to align themselves with the protesters. When they realised there was no progress with their applications, they too asked for help and filled in the appropriate forms. They had felt justified in their cases, because of fears of being persecuted for their religious beliefs. That was no guarantee of automatic acceptance, as many would realise later, when their case officers and the Refugee Review Tribunal would reject them.

One of the Sabian Mandean families was more fortunate. I met Masoud and his wife, Hamidh, and their 13-year-old son, Youhana, and 12-year-old daughter, Seemen. They were a delightful and charming family. Masoud explained how many of the Sabian Mandeans had been denied the usual occupations in Iran and had become goldsmiths, as Masoud had, or silversmiths. Masoud's faith was very real. He believed God had led them to Australia. On one occasion, after seeing a video on the Great Barrier Reef, he went into raptures about God's creative handiwork. His son, Youhana, volunteered to help in the classroom and lapped up the English lessons. I feared for them, like the other Sabian Mandeans, but after a little more than two months the good news came through about their protection visas. Masoud was overjoyed and with a broad smile on his face went around hugging everyone.

The escapees, Amir, Aziz, Bijan, Morteza, Ali, Hamid and Javed, ran off into the bush behind Woomera. They were free and 'felt like birds', Aziz would recall later. They walked close to the road, making their way to a small town, Pimba, to the south. When a car passed they retreated into the bush. At Pimba, from their hiding place near a train, they saw two police cars going back and forth through the town and, at one stage, could hear police voices.

The police set up roadblocks on the Stuart Highway and on the road to Roxby Downs.

When the police left, Morteza, who had been so quiet and studious in the library, volunteered to see which of the two trains standing on the tracks would move first. After half an hour Morteza returned to say that he thought maybe one would move off. He was wrong—the other one moved off instead.

Javed managed to jump aboard a truck that took him to Port Augusta. A van driver picked him up walking by the side of the road on the outskirts of Port Augusta. The men could not under-stand each other but the driver took Javed to someone who might help him in Adelaide. The driver's friend looked after him for a while, giving him a shower, some clothes and food. Javed was able to contact his brother in Sydney and later two men came to the house to pick him up. He reached Sydney and then decided it was pointless; he gave himself up at Merrylands police station.

The others moved off to Spud's restaurant attached to the Pimba service station. They thought that maybe they could hitch a ride on a truck. One eventually came into the service station and Bijan jumped on to the back. The truck suddenly pulled out leaving the others stranded. Bijan jumped off the truck when it reached Port Pirie and then managed to catch a bus to Adelaide. In Adelaide he persuaded a Palestinian businessman to give him some food and money for a bus ticket to Melbourne. The money was ten dollars less than the cost of the ticket. The ticket seller became suspicious and informed the police. The police were waiting for Bijan when he returned that evening to catch the bus. The businessman was fined $120 for assisting Bijan. Bijan ended up in Yatala, Adelaide's main jail. After a few days, Javed joined him from Sydney.

The other five stayed in a culvert for the night. Helicopters flew overhead and it began to rain. They moved to the back of a truck loaded with lucerne hay, parked near Spud's restaurant. During the second night at Pimba they ventured outside; they were very cold and had had no food and water. Their meagre ration of honey from the mess and chocolate unwittingly given to them by Pam, had all gone. They returned to the railway track to find a wagon that had a container large enough to conceal them. Morteza, Ali and Hamid managed to scramble on one of the wagons of a freight train. They had not known it was going west and how cold the journey would be. Once in Perth they asked for food and shelter at a mosque but the police were called instead. They were jailed for eight months.

The two cousins, Amir and Aziz, stayed for six nights altogether at Pimba before they decided they had had enough. They could not care less what happened to them now. They walked for about five kilometres south of Pimba before a truck driver spotted them and called the police. They were sent to Port Augusta jail and stayed there for about six weeks before being moved temporarily to Yatala Correctional Centre in Adelaide. In late August, Amir, Aziz and Bijan were sent back to the Woomera detention centre. After six months and only one interview they all felt abandoned—no-one had understood their plight. No-one had been willing to help them. DIMIA had not responded to their requests. They had wanted to let people know about their problems and so they had escaped.

Meanwhile, about this time, the Immigration Minister, Philip Ruddock, rejected as 'extraordinarily naive' a parliamentary committee's key recommendation of a 14-week time limit on the mandatory detention of illegal immigrants. The chairman of a parliamentary committee, Senator Alan Ferguson, made the recommendation after members said they were 'shocked' by what had confronted them on a nationwide tour of the Australia's detention facilities.

The committee presented its report, *A report on visits to immigration detention centres*, to both Houses of Parliament on 18 June 2001.

Concerning the length of detention the report stated:

The most constant complaint from detainees was about the length of their detention. They felt they were being held in a jail-like environment and treated as criminals. A comparison with prisoners was often made, with claims that prisoners were better off because they knew why they were in jail, were provided with better facilities and knew how long their sentence would be.

In the most soul-destroying of places, though, there can be fun and laughter. Performers Steve and Charlotte proved this with their drama, song and dance workshops to the children and adults in the Mike, November and main compounds. For two days they involved the children in their acrobatics, clowning, juggling, and song and dance routine. At the end of a workshop in the main compound, children took part in a conga accompanied by chanting from the adults. Their performances lifted the spirits of everyone attending.

Back to reality and two green screens were put up to prevent any communication between Oscar and November compounds and the main compound. Shortly after, an incident occurred where a security officer was alleged to have stomped on the Koran and thrown it. The rock throwing and chanting began mid-morning and went on to noon. The door to our office was midway between the compounds and, as I stepped out, some rocks landed close by. The water cannon had already moved into place and took the impact of most of the rocks. Then we had lunch, to the chanting of 'Allahu akbar' (God is great). Sharon commented how bizarre and surreal it was that we should be having lunch in the midst of this slinging and shouting fracas. Later, the manager was able to pacify the protesters saying that the officer would be suspended from duties pending an inquiry.

In the last week of June the medical doctor, Bernice, decided she had had enough. She cut short her one-year contract by three months. The added responsibility with very sick patients increasing in number had been overwhelming. An extra 200 more arrivals were expected that weekend and a possible 500 coming later were just too many with every service already at breaking point. It had been time to go.

Later, Bernice said:

The stress was too high for me. When I started I had a very blinkered view of the Middle Eastern people. We knew about the mandatory policy but I would confine myself to a medical assessment of people. In October 2000, the scales fell from my eyes. We had a tiny hut that could fit no more than 15 people. There were at least ten nurses along with psychologists, social workers and interpreters.

Many people came with chronic conditions like asthma, diabetes and high blood pressure. As well there were cases of tuberculosis, typhoid, scabies and diseases contracted while travelling to Australia. We could treat all of these but the things we found difficult were the immense stress, severe signs of depression and anxiety— even to the level of psychosis.

Then there were the hunger strikes, the continual slashings and the attempts at hanging. When you're inside you can see the stages that lead to these conditions. They are constantly living in limbo, losing self-esteem, dignity and almost humanity. The security officers weren't used to looking after people in these kinds of situations; they treated the detainees in a very authoritarian and dismissive way. There was a horrendous build up of a call for help and the actions of the detainees showed an involuntary and uncharacteristic response to a high level of stress. As far as their processing, they were left in limbo—given no record of progress or what status they were.

When you had visitors the house was swept clean. We have tried to work behind the scenes.

(14 May 2002, Australian Refugee Association Forum— *How Detention affects Asylum Seekers*, Underdale Campus of the University of South Australia)

Darryl, the psychologist, was of a similar mind to Bernice and terminated his one-year contract after three months. He had received legal advice to leave because of the increased professional risk associated with the inability to look after high-risk patients.

The mood of the main compound dramatically lifted the following Tuesday with the release of 31 detainees. DIMIA notified everyone well in advance so there was ample opportunity to say goodbye. As each person made his or her way to Golf Three gate there were lots of hugs, cheers and well-wishing. Zeyad, our computer manager, who had so ably taken over from Amir, was one of them. As I shook hands and wished him the best as a graphics designer, he said, 'I love you like a brother.'

Geeta, our English teacher who wrote the article on Peace for the newsletter, also left. Inese gave her a big hug and both started sobbing. And two of the cheeriest teenage girls, Zahra and Zainab, also left—they seemed to ride through every day with a smile on their faces. How could they do that?

On release days, Tuesdays and Thursdays, it was common practice for the programs staff who had close contact with the detainees to go to the assembly point for departure. Strictly speaking we were not allowed to visit them there but usually the security staff turned a blind eye. It lifted our spirits to see people go.

Fifteen Pentium 3 computers arrived for Mike and November compounds and five more for the main compound so I looked around for detainees with computer expertise to manage the centres. Zeyad was almost irreplaceable with the efforts he had put in teaching and keeping the computers functioning. Majid, a 23-year-old from Iran, had some experience with computers and was keen to look after the computers in the main compound.

The computers were a great boon and in heavy demand. They provided a much needed interest. But 30 computers in four compounds were not enough. We tried to be as fair as possible to give everyone at least an hour a day. The numbers kept coming so we allowed two per computer and a swap over after half an hour. Some were so keen they came in their lunchtime.

Majid was a Sabian Mandean and said that Muslims had harassed him in Iran. Tom Atherton, a former Uniting Church minister at Woomera, described on *Encounter* (Radio National, 21 January 2001) how he discovered these Baptists of the desert:

> So it became my congregation in some measure. And they're lovely, lovely people. Traditionally, Sabians are pacifists and vegetarians. But the Sabians are trying to get out of Iran and Iraq to practise their religion freely. They are under a degree of extreme difficulty in those two countries. And if only one-tenth of their stories are true they've had a horrendous background.

As a Sabian Mandean, Majid said he had been denied basic rights and could not go to university or work for the Government. Instead, he started his own business as a gold seller. He could not practise his religion freely and was constantly scared that he and his family would be assaulted. His father died because the doctors had refused to treat him in hospital. Also, his sister had to leave school because the authorities tried to force her to convert to Islam. The authorities closed the Mandean Church in his home town because it was not recognised. Majid dated a Muslim girlfriend and they wanted to marry. Because of their relationship, the girl's brother and father pushed her off the balcony of their home, causing her to break her arm and hip. They also went to Majid's house and beat up his mother and brother. The girl's family then threatened to kill Majid to clear the 'shameful matter' and to clear their family name. Majid could not see his girlfriend again so he decided to sell some gold and pay a smuggler to help him leave Iran.

As well as the Sabian Mandeans, about 10 per cent of the asylum seekers had a Christian background. They included about 50 Assyrian Christians from Iraq who had a unique culture, language and heritage, some Armenians from Iran and three Vietnamese Catholics. Some detainees had taken all the steps to be received into the Catholic Church, including baptism and confirmation, and others were at different stages of receiving instruction.

Three chaplains looked after the Christians and there was some contact from the Persian Evangelical Christian Church in Sydney. There did not appear to be any proselytising of the Christian faith. Some of the Iranians, though, questioned the chaplains about a God who could possibly love and forgive. As far as their application for a visa was concerned, the case officer would have to be convinced that their Christian conversion was genuine and that the fear of persecution in their own country was well-founded. For the latter, the credibility of their claims would be tested against background reports collected by Country Information Services (CIS) from their countries describing current and past events with respect to any kind of persecution.

By the beginning of July the number of detainees was over 1100—everyone was stretched to the limit. In every section we needed more officers and ACM started training raw recruits to fill the void. The security officers were especially affected and it was easy to see why some were going on stress leave. Extra staff were needed at the gates to help control the movement of detainees and to cope with the increased demands. They decided to go on a 'go slow' protest to bring their plight to the attention of ACM. The medical staff had to cover routine tests of detainees on arrival as well as handle everyday patients—their normal working days were 12-hour shifts. The psychologists had to deal with a host of mental problems, including those with suicidal tendencies.

Once the detainees had passed through their three interviews they moved into the main compound. With the overcrowding came a volume of complaints, especially relating to the inadequacies of the showers and toilets. Rumours were circulating that some of the women would avoid going into the toilets by not drinking. Then there were the unwelcome queues for mealtimes—with three sittings lunchtime could last for three hours. And there could be a long wait for medical attention and for the issue of items such as soap, toothpaste, tampons and disposable nappies.

Often the detainees had to contend with the cramped confines of their donga. Rezai, one of the detainees, said he shared a donga, eight metres by three and a half metres, with 16 other men. A security officer would shine a torch in the night to make sure of the tally and that those who were being closely observed were all right. 'People would wake up in the middle of the night screaming. Woomera is a place that tears your mind, your personality and your dignity,' Rezai said.

Along with the help given by the psychologists, Father Jim and Sister Anne of the local Catholic Church were always available for counselling, as well as running services for the Christian community. Sister Dot, from the Catholic Church in Gawler, wanted to find out for herself what was going on and was keen to help in any practical way. Having obtained permission from the manager, Sister Dot, my wife Liz, and I visited the centre on a Sunday.

Sister Dot's first impression on seeing the Woomera centre had been one of disbelief. She said she couldn't believe this could this be happening in our country. After entering through the five-metre high gates we passed by Oscar compound and stopped at November compound to say hello to a few of the detainees close to the fence. We moved on to Mike compound where there was little activity, then over to India compound, and by the kitchen and medical centres before calling up Haman through the public-address system to come over to Golf Three gate of the main compound. Haman was expecting us and soon arrived. He was not allowed to come out so we talked through the fence for a few minutes under the watchful eye of the security officer. Other detainees started to mill around and the security officer shouted at them to move on. We finished our quick tour with a look at the administrative block, where we met the intelligence officer who advised us to complete our visit within five minutes because of some unrest within one of the compounds. Dot said later:

> The silence got to me when we went in. Everyone walked so slowly. One man had something in his hands—a string of beads—and walked up and down the fencing. When we walked in further it reminded me of the cattle sales. These were human beings like us. Then there was a sign of dignity as they talked to us, and some of them called out, 'Hello, Mr Tom.' In the main compound the men were isolated groups. Where were the women and children? There were only a couple of kids kicking a ball. I didn't see any families together. It was the barrenness of it all. Why put them out in the never-never?

Sister Dot would never forget her visit—it was indelibly impressed into her soul. She thought a lot about what was happening in her own country. She was only one voice and felt powerless but she rallied support from people in Gawler. They responded with books, hundreds of magazines, toys, sewing materials and balls of wool that were handed over to the detainees via the recreational officers. Other people, on hearing about the needs, responded in a similar way.

My wife, Liz, was also horrified at the way in which the asylum seekers were confined. She also could not believe that this was happening in Australia. Others were as deeply affected as Sister Dot and Liz. Not long after, four Adelaide University law students conducted interviews with asylum seekers at the detention centre. One of them commented that they had been warned but nothing could have prepared them for the isolation, imprisonment and degradation of the detainees.

Two new teachers arrived to assist us—Lyn, a teacher from Adelaide and Leon, a social psychologist and a professor of gerontology. Inese took Lyn under her wing and Leon tagged along with me for the first day. A large class of over 80 new arrivals, men and women, came into the mess in Mike compound and with the help of an Iraqi woman, Sabcha, who spoke Arabic and Farsi, we sorted them out into beginners and advanced classes for learning English. With five teachers we divided up the children and adults: Inese would be responsible for most of the unaccompanied minors, now numbering more than 60, and attend to Oscar compound; Leon would look after some unaccompanied minors as well as looking after men and women in Mike compound and the main compound; Sarah would still look after her 'littlies'; Lyn would attend to the 8–12s in Mike compound and the main compound as well as take some adult women; and I would look after the 8–12s and advanced English for adults in the November and main compounds as well as look after the three computer centres, library and kindergarten, and oversee the assistant teachers for the beginner groups.

Haman came back to help us, having recovered somewhat from his depression. Three Afghani detainees also took beginner classes—Amani, Aref and Yazdan. In addition, Frederic, a new arrival from Iraq, spoke English well and took classes. I expressed some amazement to Amani, from Kabul, as to why so many people were coming to English classes. Some of the Afghanis were so keen that they were coming to both the beginners and advanced classes. He said, 'The Afghan people had a tradition of learning and they have been denied this because of the Taliban. Now they are trying to make up for lost time.'

Altogether, we were running about 35 one-hour classes a day for children and adults in all the compounds. About 85 per cent (180) of the children were coming to lessons and 35 per cent (335) of adults were attending. Without the help of about 30 English-speaking detainees we could not run all the classes for both children and adults. In March we had three hours' contact a day with the children but by the middle of July—even with five teachers—we had to reduce the contact time for children to one to two hours a day because of the lack of classrooms. Peter, the centre manager, was happy with those figures and said they were about right for detention centres. I was not so happy but if more adults came along to classes we could not cope without more classrooms and more teachers.

Fortunately, while the children missed out on teaching, the recreational officers came to the rescue in providing other types of activities—sport, art, music, song and dance, board games, children's club and even an occasional excursion.

Flexibility was the name of the game—never knowing from one day to the next whether the assistant detainee teachers would turn up; they might be shifted to a new compound, released, or they might have an appointment with DIMIA or the health centre. The classes for beginners would start off from scratch with the basic ABC, simple reading and conversational exercises.

For the advanced, there were graded conversational exercises—everyone joined in. Right from the outset we talked in simple terms about Australia and then each State separately. With the help of maps of the States showing the capitals, towns, geographical features, resources and industries, they conversed in pairs, one asking questions about each State and the other replying. We would spend a little time in each lesson on new vocabulary before devoting the rest to Australian life skills. And some asked to speak 'Strine' so we learned how to say some of the more common expressions such as 'g'day' and 'fair dinkum'. One of the idioms they learned was 'Buckley's chance'. Aref, one of our teachers, was always using it, especially in relation to the visa, so I cooled his enthusiasm a bit by saying we did not really use the phrase that often.

Aref, a 47-year-old Pushtun, from Jalalabad, in Afghanistan, had an easygoing manner in his teaching and the Afghanis responded well to him. He was always cheerful with a twinkle in his eye. He hobbled along with one leg shorter than the other. He had been appointed as an agronomist from 1974 to 1983 and then as a farm manager from 1984 to 1991 of a large irrigation development project in Nangrahar province. The 3000-hectare farm was impressive even by Australian standards, with 750 dairy and beef cows, 1200 hectares of sweet orange, grapefruit and lemon, 300 hectares of olive trees and a nursery for propagating 40,000 citrus and olive seedlings. In addition, they grew wheat, barley, sorghum and lucerne. Aref had supervised 1200 staff in multi-disciplinary teams for running the various enterprises. In 1981 his vehicle went over a landmine that exploded, causing extensive damage to his foot.

While the Russians occupied Afghanistan there was no security. Later, when they came into power, the Mujahideen stole everything from the farm, including the farm machinery.

Aref also held the position of director of irrigation and water supply for Nangrahar province from 1989 to 1992. He supervised a workforce of 120 staff, managing the reconstruction of dams and cleaning canals. Due to the unstable government in Afghanistan, Aref worked with Médecins Sans Frontières for some months in south-west Afghanistan, as an administration assistant, helping to provide primary health care to mothers and children.

Because Aref worked in former government departments he was suspected of both anti-Mujahideen and anti-Taliban activities. In addition, while living in Jalalabad, Aref and his wife, a nurse, was identified by the Taliban as working for human rights— for freedom of women—and teaching children in their home. Soon after, Aref knew that his life was in danger and decided to hide in Kabul, leaving behind his wife and six children. The Taliban, though, discovered and arrested him. He spent 20 days in a cell with only one glass of water and a small portion of bread each day. During the night he heard screams from other inmates while they were being whipped and beaten. He himself was kicked during the day. With the lack of water, he developed kidney problems. He screamed and called for treatment. The Taliban eventually allowed him to visit a doctor who happened to be a friend of his. While the guards waited outside, he escaped through a window, ran to a wealthy friend's house and hid there for 10 days. His friend then paid A\$7000 for smuggling him out of Afghanistan into Pakistan and on to an unknown country.

Aref's flight route took him from Peshawar to Karachi, where he learned he would be going to Australia. From Karachi he flew to Thailand and on to Jakarta for 14 days. Five buses took 200 people during the night to a coastal destination ready for boarding an eight-metre boat for Christmas Island. After 52 hours at sea, they neared Christmas Island and an Australian naval vessel met them. An officer asked: 'Why are you coming here? Do you have an Australian passport?' No-one replied.

Aref spoke English but was too seasick and kept quiet at first. Then he mustered up some courage and said, 'We have come from Afghanistan. We want you to accept us as refugees.'

They stayed on the boat for one more night and were provided with water. After three days on Christmas Island they flew to Adelaide, and then to Woomera. When Aref saw the high fence at Woomera he thought he would stay in this prison for two or three days until cleared.

Once a week at least I would show a video about life in Australia. It helped to reinforce what the detainees had learned. Some of the favourites were: *Australia*, *Australian Wildlife*, *Crocodile Hunter*, *Bush Tucker Man* and *The Great Barrier Reef.* Word soon got around that I would be showing a video the next day. The classroom would only take 30 but usually for the showings we packed in about 50 before turning the rest away for a promised re-run. On one occasion I showed a video on the history of the Ghan, the famous train from Adelaide to Alice Springs. The Afghanis loved it. It was a link with their past as they saw how their forebears, as 'camel-men' had helped build the Ghan and open up the outback.

I asked from time to time why a detainee who did not speak English would not come along to learn and the usual response was that he or she was too depressed after their case had been rejected. Some even said they would learn once they were released. And some of the young men were perhaps more interested in playing soccer, which clashed with classes in the afternoon. Whatever the reasons, we really needed to find out if we could do anything about encouraging more adults. Three months or more in a detention centre provided a golden opportunity to learn English and acquire Australian life skills that would give them an excellent start for living, studying and working in Australia.

With regards to the unaccompanied minors, Inese had a tough job trying to look after them. Many of them needed extra attention and support that we could not provide. As a teenage group they were more in need of help than others, especially if there were to be any hope of them fitting into Australian society. We needed extra carers and teachers to encourage them to learn English and to acquire life skills. Inese attended the weekly management meeting to discuss the special needs of the unaccompanied minors, but she felt the management was doing only the required minimum in terms of support.

When an unaccompanied minor was released, FAYS would assist in finding a foster family. Inese informed me that FAYS support staff would have liked free access to the centre but could do so only when an incident such as physical abuse had been reported. Emotional abuse was not such an incident.

In Mike compound, Jamshid, an Iranian Christian, was only too willing to help with any interpreting, as well as looking after the computer centre there. He and his pregnant wife, Ashraf, were hoping to be released soon. After two months and only one interview it did not look promising. We loaded up the English and typing programs into the computers and soon he was in full swing conducting adult classes.

For the new compounds, Mike and November, Pam organised a mobile library; it was barely adequate but better than nothing. Dictionaries, magazines and books were snapped up and many never returned. The officers in charge of property carried out a search on the belongings of the detainees being released and we recovered some that way. Meanwhile, Irene and Sonia arranged daily activities such as craft, art, painting, sewing, table tennis and games. Many of the men preferred not to engage in these types of activities or even come to classes for learning English. Although the facilities for teaching and activities were really inadequate for everyone, it was difficult to know how limiting they were, given the depressed state of many of the adults.

A game of soccer worked wonders and, while the youngsters and young men joined in, many welcomed an opportunity to watch from the sidelines. The afternoon soccer game attracted a lot of interest in the main compound and by about five o'clock the men had come out of their dongas. The teams played each other with great zest—especially if there was an international game—the players shouting and scrambling as fast as they could over a hard, gravelly surface. The trick was to stay on your feet as you tackled someone, otherwise you could end up in the medical centre.

About this time Sajed and his two sisters, Dina and Triza, had come back to Mike compound after being moved around over a four-month period from compound to compound. Their mother was patiently awaiting them in Perth, having come out two years before from Iraq. With no apparent progress in their case, Triza became distressed and slashed herself in front of Irene. Sajed was beside himself with concern. Later I met him, subdued and crestfallen. He said, though, that she was all right. After that, I visited them on several occasions, bringing them some books and magazines or just a word of encouragement. They usually kept to themselves in their room and Sajed, normally a bright and cheerful person, was downcast from taking on the weight of his sisters' despair.

Sajed and his sisters had fled to Teheran from Iraq and had lived there illegally with a friend of their father's. They had tried to apply to the Australian embassy for a visa but were refused entry. After one year with no progress, their friend helped in procuring false passports and they flew to Malaysia. There they met the smugglers who arranged a passage for them, along with about 60 other people, by boat to Sumatra in Indonesia. The promised journey of six hours turned into a nightmarish three days. They were crammed into the boat, huddled together with not even an opportunity to stand for fear of falling into the water. There were no toilets. Sajed did not eat or drink anything for the whole voyage. During the night it was often raining and during the day there was no protection from the sun. At one stage the captain lost the way and some of the passengers started to fight with him but there was not really enough space to have a fight so they had to calm down. They landed near Medan and then travelled by bus to the southern tip of Sumatra, where they boarded a ferry that took them across to Java, and then they travelled on to Jakarta. There they stayed in a house for two months before journeying to Lombok, from where they went by boat to Ashmore Reef. From there the Australian navy sent them by ferry to Darwin.

On a brighter note, and I think a first for detention centres, the main compound joined in the wedding celebrations of Mariam, a 24-year-old woman from Iraq, and Abdullah, a 33-year-old from Chechnya. Music, singing, dancing and clapping were heard across the compounds until 11 pm as detainees celebrated and congratulated the happy couple. The couple had met on the boat coming out from Indonesia. Their happiness was to be short-lived, though, as soon after the wedding DIMIA released Mariam but rejected Abdullah's application. Among other reasons, Abdullah's case officer apparently thought that the marriage was one of convenience.

A Vietnamese couple, Dac Cong and his wife, Nga Hang Thi, appeared on the scene. They were like fish out of water, not being able to communicate in English, Arabic or Farsi. Nga Hang Thi spoke just enough English to say they were desperate for English-Vietnamese phrase and grammar books. They were overjoyed when we found these. Not long after, Minh, another Vietnamese man arrived, looking lost with no way of communicating with anyone. He did not want to come to classes but was keen to learn English so we gave him some exercises to try on his own.

In November compound, Shahin was becoming more and more concerned for his wife, Samira, who was six months' pregnant. She was having nightmares about returning to Iran and even told Shahin that she wanted to return to buy a tomb next to her father so that she and her baby would rest in peace. He had written a letter to Philip Ruddock appealing for his mercy to allow Samira to give birth outside the detention centre. In the event, he did not send it as about a week later on 18 July DIMIA started interviews with them and others in November compound.

About this time incidents of self-harm were becoming more frequent. On 13 July, a detainee held a piece of glass to his throat. He had wanted to make a phone call. On 16 July, a detainee swallowed detergent and was treated by medical staff. On 18 July a detainee self-harmed and was put on two-minute observations. Another detainee on the same day was screened out and slashed himself.

There were a number of cases with unaccompanied minors self-harming and falling into a depressed state. Leon tried his best to encourage them and even dragged some out of bed for his morning classes. After a few times of being subjected to this indignity they soon got the message and started coming to English classes.

There were too many 5–7s and 8–12s so Sarah and Lyn had no choice but to split the classes. It meant the children would be getting only one hour's contact time per day—totally inadequate.

Someone in Federal Parliament needed to have some answers by fax about providing educational services at Woomera Immigration Reception and Processing Centre. I responded to questions such as: 'How could you manage if you increased the number of contact hours?' 'How do you manage if more want to attend classes?' 'How are classes organised?' I replied simply that more class-rooms and more teachers were necessary if we were going to teach children for half a day and the adults for more than one hour a day.

DIMIA was well aware of our teaching limitations, particu-larly with respect to the availability and type of classrooms. They came up with plans for a new school in the main compound which would cater for a population of 2000, 25 per cent of which could be children. Sarah and I examined the proposals and suggested a number of additions and changes, most of which were approved. The number of classrooms would be doubled and there would be a library, computer centre, physical education area, a resource and reading room, a kindergarten and playground. The children would have a minimum of three hours contact a day. From the plans of the new school I was able to calculate the area of the proposed school as 2000 square metres and the Woomera centre complex to be approximately eight and a half hectares.

On 13 August the Iranians came to blows with the Afghanis in the main compound. The security officers shifted most of the Iranians to November compound; Haman went to Oscar for his safety. Peter, our new teacher, wore the usual first-day stunned look.

The following day more than 50 detainees were released. Some of the remaining Afghanis threatened a demonstration the following day. It was sooner than that—in the evening some of them shook part of the fence and a gate came down on a child and broke his leg. The next day the maintenance crew was busily putting an additional roll of razor-edged wire between the inner and outer fences. The water cannons moved into position and some of the security officers put on riot gear in readiness.

Thirty detainees went on a hunger strike while they camped by the fence not far from Golf Three gate. In the afternoon, I was teaching in November when Teresa, a newly appointed teacher, appeared and said, 'Could you wind up as quickly as possible?' Now there were about 200 demonstrators in the main compound walking around the perimeter of the compound calling for DIMIA to act, and shouting, '*Allahu akbar*'. Eventually, the demonstrators dispersed—there would be more action later, I was sure.

Many of the long-term children were becoming restless and bored, not attending classes at all and getting into strife. On one occasion some of the boys jammed the padlocks to the computer centre rooms with wooden plugs. Fortunately, an Iraqi produced a forbidden tool set and managed to prise the offending pieces of wood out with a homemade gimlet. Sharon was particularly concerned about the worsening behavioural patterns of these children. 'Who knows what they have gone through before a lengthy stay here?' she said.

Mahmoud, an Iranian, and a friendly giant of a man, started to cause concern by cutting himself and jumping quite often onto the roof of one of the compound buildings. It was his way of protesting about the delay in his visa application. Each time this happened a CERT call was made to alert everyone and restrict movement.

17 August was full of drama again. I stayed back to run a computer class during the lunch hour with some keen Afghanis in the main compound. At about midday there was a lot of banging and shouting coming from Oscar. Shortly after, the noise seemed closer. I looked out of the computer room and about 25 metres away there were about 70 detainees pushing on the five-metre Golf Two gate. The gate swayed back and forth, moving five to 10 degrees off the vertical. It was going to go, I was sure. Then the water cannon moved in and the detainees decided to move back. Meanwhile, a CERT call came over the radio and everyone beat a hasty retreat out of the compound—even the security officers had sought refuge behind the protective fences. I closed up the two computer rooms. My students were reluctant to leave and were almost oblivious to what was going on—such was the power of the computer.

The crowd dispersed but reports were coming through that some of the detainees were throwing stones at windows and were tearing beds apart. Frederic was also having a lunchtime class— I had forgotten about him. They were coming out of the classroom when one of them motioned to me to stay where I was—behind the computer centre. Then after about five minutes he beckoned and this time I emerged. About 10 of them, including Frederic, formed a cohort and we walked the 120 metres to Golf Three gate. I was very moved by their compassion to protect me from possible harm. As we strode across the compound the security officers, interpreters and other officers looked on from outside. I thanked the detainees for their concern and unofficial escort. The security officer on the gate thought I should have radioed in to let them know where I was. I said I did not think I was in danger and that I was keeping the airway clear. It was not very convincing. Harold patted me on the back and Jamal thought I had been taken hostage. The programs and administrative staff were in the mess awaiting further instructions. The security staff then told us to go back to Woomera township.

I was a little jumpy the next time I heard an outcry and that was only three days later. While teaching in Mike compound there was a lot of whooping and shouting. It was Sajed and his two sisters—Marie had just given them the news that after six months they were free to go to Perth to rejoin their mother. Triza, who had twice harmed herself, jumped up and down with joy and was hugging everyone in sight. Dina had tears in her eyes. Sajed and I hugged and I wished them all the best. In parting, he said, 'I'll never forget you. I'll never forget your classes.'

Often in between classes, at lunchtime or at the end of the day I would try to cope with the many requests. Some wanted simple things such as writing paper or a dictionary. Some were after specific reading materials, such as Farsi or Arabic stories, medical journals for doctors or magazines for computer-trained people. Magazines about families, homes, cooking, Australia and sport were very popular. The Woomera library was happy to help out wherever possible. Some requests were harder to fulfil—such as finding a cassette of Kurdish music for a small number of Kurds, or a recorder for an Afghani. And some were almost impossible—such as supplying a radio or cassette player. As well, there were contraband items such as cigarettes. I bought a cigarette lighter, though, and the detainees often approached me for a light. It was a good way of getting to know some I had never met before.

Often, a small group of two or three would approach and just wanted to talk. There was always someone who acted as an interpreter. At other times detainees wanted help with understanding a legal document or the reasons why their case for a visa had been rejected. Over the course of six months I talked to many about their cases and helped to clarify some of the wording in their case documents.

An unexpected request came from Zeyad, our ex-computer man, who was trying to settle in Sydney. I had given him my mobile number and he rang to introduce Mr Al-Hashimy, whose wife and four children were in November compound. I was able to reassure him that they were all doing well. Asra'a, Ahmed and Zainab were bright and keen students. Then Mr Al-Hashimy decided to see his family with his private lawyer, Dr Mohamed Al Jabiri. Mr Al-Hashimy had come to Australia nearly two years before and had spent almost the first year in Port Hedland detention centre before being granted a temporary protection visa. It was quite common, I discovered, for husbands to come first, followed by their families. The granting of a TPV to a husband did not have any bearing on the decision-making process by DIMIA for his wife and children. Each case was considered separately and as a result the wives and children would often be kept in detention for many months. And in the Bakhtiari case the door had closed altogether for any hope of Roqia, and her children, being reunited with her husband, Ali, who had been granted a TPV.

After the reunion I met Dr Jabiri and Mr Al-Hashimy in the Eldo Hotel. Dr Jabiri had an intimate knowledge of many cases and of the situation in Iraq. He spoke about the inequities in processing the cases of applicants and reasons for discrepancies and inconsistencies in their accounts. As we parted, Mr Al-Hashimy insisted I have $50 to buy his family sweets, crisps and chocolates. What could I do? I consoled myself that 'never show favouritism' was never going to work. I smuggled the food items into the centre over a number of visits and enjoyed watching the children's response.

Oscar Compound

Many requests came from the long-term residents in Oscar compound (formerly named Sierra). Most were single men and had been there for more than eight months, with the longest 20 months. Conditions were never good in any of the compounds but in Oscar there were more privileges, such as a room to oneself and access to TV and newspapers.

By the middle of July there were 41 detainees in Oscar— 26 Iranians, six Iraqis, three Tunisians, three Moroccans, one Palestinian, one Afghani and one Russian. All of them knew they were in for a hard battle ahead with their cases—they usually dragged on much longer than those in the other compounds. In some cases Iranians were kept in limbo for more than six months before their second interview, and in Haman's case more than seven months.

As a result of the prolonged waiting, the detainees in Oscar compound reacted adversely—there were many cases of dysfunctional behaviour, self-mutilation and attempted suicide. Surprisingly, through all the difficulties they faced, there was a bonding and a camaraderie that were not so obvious in the other compounds.

Inese was looking after the English classes in Oscar. She struck a rapport with the detainees and involved herself in far more than the mere teaching of English. There were some distressing cases of slashings and attempted hangings in July that affected her. Inese was more than a teacher—she listened, advised and empathised with their plight.

In the last two weeks of July a CERT call was made on most days, as a result of incidents in Oscar. On 17 July one who had slashed himself was sent to Adelaide. Two detainees tried to hang themselves on 20 July—one of them was sent to Adelaide for treatment. A number of staff commented that it was hard to imagine how no-one had taken their own life. It was also difficult to comprehend that these events occurred almost daily and were causing barely a ripple.

By 24 July there were two more attempted hangings in Oscar, more slashings and one detainee attempted suicide by burning a mattress while he lay beneath it. Someone noticed the fire and raised the alarm. The detainee pulled through after treatment for his burns. His room was gutted and blackened so much on the outside that it provided a chilling reminder of what could have happened if he had not been discovered.

All of this was too much for Inese and by the end of July she complained of pains in her chest. Two days later and two weeks short of her contract, Australasian Correctional Management advised her to leave so she could receive proper medical attention in Adelaide. It was sad to see her leave under these circumstances after she had put in so much effort with the women and unaccompanied minors in the other compounds, as well as the men in Oscar.

Some of the interpreters and recreational officers really put themselves out to help those in Oscar and some broke a few rules in the process. Pam, like Inese, was a helpful one and could not do enough for them. She often broke down crying when she heard about a rejection or an attempted suicide—it was too much for her. Others, such as Rosetta, Sigrid and Farah, on the recreational side, always tried to visit Oscar and spent as much time as possible with those there. The men, having no contact otherwise with women, appreciated their friendliness. Unfortunately, ACM viewed their contact as being over-friendly and for a while they were barred from Oscar.

The Farsi interpreters, Mehrdad, Nadir and Shaheen, and the Arabic ones, Jamal, Frossine and Mary, also could not do enough to ease the plight of the detainees, especially those in Oscar compound. Mehrdad, a veteran at Woomera detention centre, seemed to be weighed down by the despair of the Iranians in particular. He worked long hours, smoked non-stop and zipped around as though a young lad on a skateboard. It took its toll though; he ran himself down, mentally and physically, becoming rakishly thin. Occasionally, our paths would meet and we had quite a number of revealing talks. He knew more than most about what was really going on—the peculiar cases of different detainees, a processing system fraught with inconsistencies and the inflexibility and lack of compassion shown towards desperate individuals and families.

About this time I managed to find some time in the afternoon to visit some of the men in Oscar. I went in under the guise of taking some English classes but really set out to talk to various detainees and find out what was happening.

I talked to Habib who was a long-term detainee in Oscar; he had not progressed beyond the first interview for six months. Then finally there was a breakthrough and he had his second and third interviews. He was typical of some of the Iranians who had left for religious reasons. Often he would approach me and talk to me about his case or the hope he had for a visa to start a new life. Always friendly, he would wave or shout to me as I passed by the kitchen where he worked during the day.

Habib was a single 28-year-old man and a Christian. He was born in Khozestan Province of Iran where he had lived until 1990. He moved to Ahvaz, and after completing 12 years of education in 1991, he undertook compulsory military service from 1992 to 1994. Then he was employed as a gardener with the Iranian National Oil Company for four months. He said his employment was terminated because he did not participate in Islamic prayers and religious ceremonies. He then drove a bus for five years. He became interested in Christianity and attended scripture classes. Habib decided to leave Iran in December 2000 because, he said, of his fear of being persecuted for his conversion and arrived in Australia three weeks later. He was not granted a visa though, after his three interviews, because there was no evidence he had been proselytising or that he had received any adverse attention from the Iranian authorities while a Christian. His case officer apparently regarded him as a low-profile Christian and relatively free to worship privately without fear of persecution. Habib appealed to the RRT.

Another Christian, Bahram, had arrived in Australia from Iran on 26 March 2000. He had been at Woomera for 18 months. He had run a sales and repairs shop for motorcycles in Iran. In 1989 there had been an argument between his family and a neighbour who had worked in the intelligence service. Bahram was shot in the elbow—this was confirmed in Australia by x-ray which showed metal shrapnel in the soft tissues of the elbow—and taken to hospital for medical treatment before going to prison. There, the officers beat him with cables and tied his arms between his legs like a chicken and continued to torture him with metal bars. After his release, Bahram found that the renewal of his business registration was difficult because he had a record with the intelligence service. Bahram said that in 1990 the religious police had caused the death of his fiancée in a head-on collision. His fiancee had worn make-up and that was why the police had forced her car into the path of a minibus. In 1999 he left his business. A friend advised him that he was on a wanted list as an activist who had participated in university riots in Teheran. Fearing execution if he were caught, Bahram went into hiding for six months and then decided to leave Iran for Australia.

Bahram became a Christian and was baptised at Woomera. He became a faithful member of the Christian group in Oscar compound. While Bahram could not legitimately claim his Christian faith as a reason for leaving Iran, he felt he would face persecution if someone passed this information on to the authorities. The Refugee Review Tribunal (RRT) did not believe, though, that there was any real basis to fear persecution on his return to Iran—he did not have an adverse political profile. The Tribunal had affirmed the decision not to grant Bahram a protection visa.

The RRT also refused a claim by Rahim, a 30-year-old Iranian, on religious grounds. He had been in Woomera detention centre for about 12 months when he told me his story. Rahim had lived in Ahvaz and Abadan and had an engineering degree. Following his military service, he had been employed in various construction companies. Rahim said his problems began in school when he raised questions about Islamic orthodoxy. At university, he had continued to criticise religious practices. Then, after his military service, he ran into similar problems with government-based employers. He was sacked for not praying as he should, as a Muslim. In 1999 he decided to start his own business but early in 2000 the Iranian intelligence arrested him for having a copy of a critique of the book *Satanic Verses*. They believed he had a copy of *Satanic Verses*. He was accused of being a *mortad*, a non-believer and apostate. He could be executed according to Islamic law. After being released he feared for his safety when he was put under surveillance. His family became worried about him and encouraged him to leave Iran. He obtained a false Iraqi passport and flew to Malaysia before travelling on to Indonesia and Australia. He became a Christian at the Woomera detention centre. The RRT did not believe that Rahim had a well-founded fear arising out of the incident with the *Satanic Verses* or from any other activities relating to religious or political issues.

Rahim was one of the more articulate English speakers of the detainees. He could communicate what others only felt. He explained that many who were in Oscar found it hard. Some tended to bottle it up inside themselves; others slashed their bodies or smashed objects.

'It's like a concentration camp here,' Rahim once said.

I told him that it was a bit severe to compare what the Nazis did in the 1940s to what was happening here.

Rahim replied:

No way. The Nazis tortured and killed the Jews. Here it is the same—they are trying to kill our spirit to live, our hope for life—our freedom. We live in the year 2001. Don't you think we should be more enlightened now, 60 years on? It's just as bad. We haven't learned anything from that time.

I asked him about his treatment in Oscar.

Fifty per cent of the officers treat us humanely; 50 per cent treat us like criminals. The people who put us here, they are the criminals; they are keeping us here unlawfully. I've wasted one year of my life. Why? Why do the Government hate us? We just want to start a new life. If you don't want us, send us back. Three months is long enough in this concentration camp.

One of the detainees, I found in Oscar, had been very upset as a result of watching the ABC *Four Corners* program on the case of the six-year-old, Shayan Badraie, who had been in detention for 17 months, first at Woomera and then at Villawood detention centre, where he had completely withdrawn from life. I too had seen the program and barely recognised him as the lad I had known in the classroom. At Woomera, Shayan had seen security officers beating detainees with batons during riots. And at Villawood, Shayan had not spoken since he had seen blood pouring from the wrists of a detainee who had tried to commit suicide. He also refused to eat or drink and had to be taken to hospital every few days for rehydration.

Aamer Sultan, a medical practitioner, and also a detainee from Iraq, had identified Shayan's condition as immigration-detention stress syndrome. *The Lancet*, a British medical journal, had published Aamer's research findings. On seeing the *Four Corners* report, the national president of the United Nations Association, Professor Margaret Reynolds, demanded a strong response. She said the plight of child refugees was a national disgrace and must no longer be tolerated by fair-minded Australians. The removal of Shayan to a foster home after the trauma of detention would only exacerbate the child's condition and further distress his family.

In general, though, I found that children showed remarkable resilience at first while in the Woomera detention centre and fared better than their parents who 'weathered' more rapidly when their cases were rejected or when they suffered lengthy delays in pro-cessing. After about six months, the children too started to succumb to their environment, no doubt reflecting their parents' malaise and dysfunction. The long-term effects of already traumatised chil-dren witnessing such riots, self-harming and spot-checking by guards in the night were not known. What happens to families like Shayan's in the long run? Will the children be separated only after suffering irreversible damage? Where can the family go if their own country does not accept them?

On 13 August, ABC's *Health Report* discussed these issues, including Shayan's state. Patrick McGorry, a Melbourne professor and an internationally recognised psychiatrist, had worked with asylum seekers since the 1980s. He found that most severely ill people had been well when they arrived but had deteriorated over time with no specialist care; some were mere shadows of their former selves. Together with Dr Zachary Steel, a clinical psychol-ogist at the University of New South Wales, they carried out research on the wellbeing of detainees. They found from their surveys that for major depressive illnesses, often running at about 90 per cent, there was a strong association with the length of stay and risk of worsening symptoms. Dr Steel stated that the trauma that the detainees had already experienced before coming to Australia was compounded by the policy of mandatory detention. The process had no mechanism for release of these people regard-less of their mental state. As a result they continued to deteriorate quite rapidly in the detention environment. They also found that there was no easing of symptoms for those with extreme disability and who had eventually been released.

In the waiting game of the close-knit environment of Oscar, being kept in limbo with a lack of communication from DIMIA took its toll. Cases went on for months through all possible legal avenues; some successful and some doomed to rejection and despair for the applicants.

Some of the programs staff felt so concerned about the people in

Oscar that they rallied to support them in their hearing with the Refugee Review Tribunal. They carefully examined their case histories for weak points that would have gone against them in the primary decision. After eliciting information in Farsi or Arabic it was translated into English and then polished as a submission to the RRT. The budding legal assistants achieved some success with at least eight visas granted after the RRT hearing. On each successful occasion the spirits of Oscar detainees lifted dramatically, if only for a short spell.

Meanwhile, Leon was trying to implement a social psychological approach in the provision of integrated social development and care services at the Woomera detention centre. One of the pressing problems identified by Leon was people in Oscar displaying symptoms of chronic social loss syndrome. His plan called for the integration of medical care and program support services— a more proactive approach than the hitherto reactive and separate approach of the different services. His approach would offer some means of coping for both officers and detainees in Oscar as well as in other compounds.

The last week

In my last week the pendulum of emotions favoured some and not others. Majid was heartbroken with his refusal by the RRT. The tribunal concluded that because he was a Mandean, the degree of actual difficulty Majid faced fell short of persecution, and that his alleged relationship with a Muslim girlfriend had been mostly made up. Parvin, our vibrant English teacher, and also a Mandean, reacted to this outcome by pacing up and down the wire fence. She, too, was having her battle as she had lived in Indonesia for about one year and needed police clearance from there.

Shahin and his wife, Samira, received their visas—I could not believe their good fortune. I was very happy for them and tracked them down to the property office to wish them all the best. They had a choice of going to Adelaide or Darwin. I told them that they must start off in Adelaide—it was cheaper and Shahin would have a reasonable chance of finding a job.

Mehrzad, who had become a Christian, had his visa application rejected—the case officer apparently did not believe that his conversion was genuine. He took it well and applied for a RRT hearing.

Meanwhile, the mood in Oscar deteriorated—one man was nearly successful at hanging himself and another slashed himself deeply with glass.

Haman moved into Oscar after seven months at the detention centre. Eight months would lapse before his second and third interviews. He was very subdued—I worried about what would become of him. Amir, our computer manager and escapee, was thinking about going back to Iran. He requested his old job back in the main compound and Peter, the centre manager, agreed.

With regard to the young ones, DIMIA also released Ali Akber, an unaccompanied minor, computer whiz and protégé of Zeyad. Giving him a responsibility in running classes and looking after the computers in the main compound kept his fertile mind alive. His cheerful attitude always prevailed, despite waiting more than six months for a visa. DIMIA granted a visa to Zia, a 12-year-old boy, and his family. Zia would meet me at the Golf Three gate and offer to help carry my load to the classroom. He often volunteered to clean the classrooms. Mahmood, a 13-year-old unaccompanied minor, always so willing to help, had no word on his case after more than eight months. Anwar Ali, now 18 and no longer an unaccompanied minor, had his RRT refusal after more than eight months. While awaiting the Federal Court decision, he decided to help out in the sewing room.

In my last two weeks a new lot of arrivals, mostly Iraqis, had come. There were altogether about 1400 detainees; 331 were children with 58 of them unaccompanied. We were down to three and half teachers; Sarah was the half, having been seconded in the afternoon to the community centre in Woomera.

A busload of new security officer recruits was going through

This and the facing page: Children's artwork

provided by Jeremy Moore

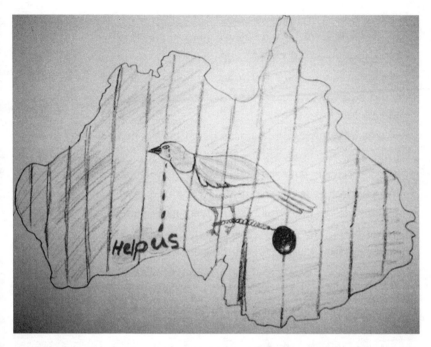

their six-week training sessions. They mostly came from nearby towns such as Woomera, Roxby Downs and Port Augusta. Two of them, Terry and Phil, had thrown in their jobs with the Woomera supermarket. It was hard to believe that these raw recruits could survive in the Woomera environment, let alone perform adequately.

The experiment of detainees living in Woomera seemed to be going well but it needed to with the amount of money allocated. The cost of setting up and running the six-month trial for 25 women and children was $1.5 million. Everyone knew it was a token response to the concerns of human rights groups. Initially, ACM and DIMIA selected five women and five children to go into a cluster of four three-bedroom houses. Most of the other eligible women refused to be separated from their husbands or friends.

Jeremy Moore, the Adelaide lawyer who had represented the detainees from the centre, commented on the trial:

> I don't think it will be very successful at all. I've spoken to people that have been at Woomera and been released and they tell me that the trauma of the family being split up will be too much and families won't agree to that proposal.

I went along to one of the houses to install some English-learning programs on the three computers. All the usual household facilities and comforts were available: there were new cooking appliances, ducted air-conditioning, a television, video recorder, toys, basic furniture, bunk beds and single beds. Four security staff seemed relaxed drinking cups of tea—relishing the change in pace and stress levels. There were a number of constraints for expanding the trial—the cost, the fears of Woomera residents, the lack of support services in the community and the reluctance of women and children to separate from a partner or father who had to stay in the centre. Staff and resources were out of all proportion to the small number of women and children. Part of the officers' duties involved escorting them for shopping and other activities as well as allowing them to visit relatives in the detention centre.

Ironically, there was enough vacant accommodation in the town of Woomera for all of Australia's detainees. The Woomera Area School, along with a Catholic primary school, could take in the school-aged children and there was even a kindergarten for the younger ones. A barely used TAFE campus could run all the English language and life skills classes. Woomera would be ideal as a halfway house before visa holders entered the Australian community equipped with some means of survival. It would never happen though.

I started off some new classes in India compound—normally only a temporary holding area for the newly arrived. There were no classrooms there so we held our classes in a recreational room. Hayat, a 33-year-old Iraqi doctor, spoke English well and acted as an interpreter.

His story was that he had begun work as an orthopaedist in a hospital when members of the Baa'th party approached him and said that he must give up his chosen profession and become a soldier in Saddam Hussein's forces. He had tried to protest but to no avail. The response was unequivocal: 'We don't need any more doctors. We need soldiers.' There had been no alternative for Hayat—he had to leave his six-month-old bride and flee Iraq.

About 60 men, women and children came along for an introductory session and with Hayat's help we divided the group up into beginners and advanced. There was great enthusiasm as everyone joined in the alphabet and simple conversational exercises. Then, after one week of enjoying their company, I had to explain to them that my contract was coming to an end.

I said goodbye to Father Jim, who, along with Sister Anne, had helped to make life in the centre a bit more bearable. Father Jim hoped I would come back again for another stint. I was not sure. He said that unfortunately we were stuck with detention centres for the time being. Father Jim described their efforts:

The role that our parish has taken is firstly to work for an improvement in conditions through various angles, and secondly to educate as many Australians as possible about the destructive realities of life in these centres for those who must live in them. We do this education through action: inviting people to be involved in lots of small actions for and on behalf of detainees which then get them thinking and talking to their family members and friends. It's only our small efforts there, but we know that there are lots of people working on various fronts for a more humane response to this overall situation.

Father Jim also said that he would be happiest if the detention centres were dismantled in favour of a community-based approach with people like myself involved up to the eyebrows in teaching, counselling, managing and the like.

Leaving the detainees behind was hard, knowing that some had little chance of being released under the current hardline policies. It was heart-rending to say goodbye to the children. Little Azita and Sapedeh, from the 8–12s class in November compound, clung to the fence and pleaded with me not to go. I said I had to—my time was up. I wished them the best and hoped they would be out soon. I dragged myself away from the November fence and stopped at nearby Oscar compound. Thamer, Adnan and Amir were there. We talked for a few minutes and I wished them the best with their cases. Both Thamer and Adnan looked skywards as they raised their arms to Allah. Amir already knew what would happen to him.

Soon after I went back to my home I heard that Haman had snapped after being rejected by his case officer. After making elaborate plans he had tried to hang himself during the night. But for the vigilance of a security officer he would have been successful. Again he tried and was saved just in time. Haman was sent to the Royal Adelaide Hospital. I rang ACM and requested permission to visit him but was refused. Then he was sent to Glenside Hospital for a few days before being sent back to the Woomera detention centre. While he was at Glenside I rang DIMIA and again I was refused permission to see him—'It is in his best interests,' the DIMIA officer said. After that, I contacted Jeremy Moore to see if he could help with Haman's case. He said he would try his best.

A FLAWED PROCESS AND
LENGTHY DELAYS

The Minister for Immigration, Philip Ruddock, replied in April 2001 to the letter which I had written about the lengthy delays in processing, putting the Government's position into context:

> The Government seeks to minimise this period of time people take to progress through the asylum determination process and, hence, the period of detention. Though significant measures have been introduced to improve the speed and effectiveness of the decision-making process and, currently, over 75 per cent of primary asylum applications are processed in six weeks, this process can take some time.
>
> The process has been aggravated by the changing composition of the people arriving illegally by boats, shifting from predominantly PRC [People's Republic of China] and Vietnamese nationals to people from the Middle East. The new composition raises far more difficult issues relating to identity, prior protection issues, possible identity fraud, criminal record checks and return arrangements. Most unauthorised arrivals enter either without documentation, having destroyed them on the way to Australia, or with fraudulent documentation and their identities are not clear.
>
> Other matters that may also extend the period in detention include delays due to litigation action and appeals, difficulties in obtaining documentation and general non-cooperation by detainees.
>
> (Ruddock April 2001)

Nothing was said with regard to a ceiling on the length of stay for asylum seekers in detention centres. In June, the Government rejected a call by a parliamentary committee that included both Liberal and Labor Members of Parliament for a 14-week time limit on the detention of asylum seekers.

On 20 November 2001 about 200 detainees rioted and caused about $140,000 in fire damage, because of the delays in the processing of cases. Six Iranians escaped for a brief time by cutting their way out with hacksaws. They were recaptured in Pimba a few hours later.

The rioting in the two weeks before Christmas 2001 was the seventh and most serious of the Woomera detention centre's two-year history. The estimate of damage due to the lighting of fires and wilful damage was close to $2 million. About 300 detainees were involved in the burning of 21 buildings. Images of flames leaping into the night sky, rampaging detainees and the wreckage of burnt buildings did not go down well with the general public.

'It was a deliberate campaign of criminal activity to hold the Australian people to ransom in order to gain visas,' a DIMIA spokesperson said.

A Woomera town spokesperson, David Kirby, commented to the media, 'It's pitch black everywhere else apart from the chanting, fires and bright lights and there's no-one to tell you if it's safe to stay.'

Jeremy Moore, the coordinating lawyer of the Woomera lawyers' group, said: 'It's a cry for help.'

The Adelaide-based Catholic social welfare director, Dale West, said: 'If you cage people, take away their hope and dignity, this is the behaviour you will get.'

A DIMIA officer said it would not bend to 'blackmail', and warned all detainees that the processing of visas would be suspended until the unrest stopped. 'Vandalism will not get people a visa,' the Acting Immigration Minister, Daryl Williams, said. 'It's entirely unsatisfactory and that's why we want to identify those responsible and remove them.'

Meanwhile the Howard Government persisted in adding fuel to the Woomera detention centre fires with its hardline response to those who were kept there for months on end by protracted legal wrangling.

After the December fires there was a new cry for help with detainees self-harming, sewing their lips together and going on hunger strikes.

Why had it come to this? Why were these outbursts of apparent wanton destruction and mutilation occurring? What could we do, if anything?

Towards the end of the year 2000 a number of the detainees who had been in the Woomera detention centre for more than nine months despaired of a positive outcome for their cases. Conditions were not conducive to a long-term stay—one of the detainees stated that you could possibly endure a three-month stay if you knew there was a definite end to all of the processing. Unfortunately, that was not the case with time-consuming legal avenues to pursue. Most detainees preferred to exhaust the full extent of these, rather than go back to their country of origin and invite what they said they feared—dishonour, arrest, imprisonment and torture. However, looming over them was the prospect of an indefinite stay with diminishing hope, in an environment that provided the basic necessities for survival but lacked a depth of compassion for traumatised people.

How could the asylum seekers have foreseen the extent of their despair? From the Howard Government's perspective, they should have checked the 1951 Refugee Convention and made sure they had a credible story and been persecuted enough with evidence and documents to support their case.

The reality, though, implied from the rhetoric, was how dare they come as uninvited guests, threatening the sanctity of our borders and security of our nation and jeopardising our planned refugee intake and humanitarian program. Reluctantly, we will give them a temporary visa, if they can prove to be eligible for refugee status. But we certainly will not give them a fair go.

The bottom line, however, was that the asylum seekers were here. Single men, widowed women, families, unaccompanied minors, some with disabilities—whatever category—all were desperate for a new beginning. Irrespective of the merits of their cases and the legitimacy of their way of coming to Australia, a compassionate response compels us to examine the whole system of mandatory detention involving conditions of confinement, treatment by staff, the quality of services provided and the processing of applicants.

For ACM it was a learning process, sped on by the concerns of humanitarian organisations and also by the detainees through their delegates within the centre. ACM responded by improving facilities for communication, education, recreation and the general welfare of detainees. I noticed a definite improvement in the quality of services and the attitudes of security officers towards detainees when I started my second contract of six months as an education officer in March 2001.

There was still a long way to go to improve conditions and services. But the new centre manager, Peter McIntosh, made a concerted effort to implement these he was open to ideas from staff and from detainee delegates. As an example, he gave full support for a computer centre for each of the three main compounds, resources for learning English and the design and implementation of plans for a new school to allow a minimum four-hour contact time a day for children. He also backed a social psychological approach to facilitate the provision of an integrated care and developmental service.

There have been complaints about the heavy-handed treatment by security officers. Generally, though, most of the officers acted professionally and, given the enormous pressure they were under, often with constant demands from detainees, it was not surprising that they sometimes reacted in an unprofessional manner. A constant complaint from the security officers was that they were understaffed.

Similarly, psychologists, medical officers, interpreters and educational officers also tried to perform their best under this constraint. It was more profitable for ACM to run with fewer staff, work them longer and harder and pay them well. The losers were the detainees who got basic services and very little extra.

Overall, conditions and services had improved at the Woomera detention centre but it was impossible to meet all the demands and requirements. Changing a one-star detention facility into a two-star one was not the answer. Ultimately, the double perimeter fence topped by razor wire was a glaring reminder of what the asylum seekers could not have.

ACM had taken a lot of the flak for detainees' suffering and frustration; it had been the scapegoat for the Department of Immigration, Multicultural and Indigenous Affairs (DIMIA). As one of the Woomera ACM senior staff described it to me, 'It's a dirty business and DIMIA has a lot to answer for.' But the DIMIA officers at Woomera had their own constraints in dealing with the processing side. The trail went right back to the Howard Government in Canberra and the policy of mandatory detention.

At Woomera, though, the 'dirty business' unfolded when you looked at some of the cases. And it was easy to see the reasons for some of the delays in the processing of applicants. The significance attached to the first interview could not be underestimated. DIMIA conducted these interviews within days of arrival. The asylum seekers were bewildered and confused and unlikely to give a clear account of the problems they had encountered in their own country. There was no legal representation for this interview and, because of this, some were screened out after it. This meant that the applicant could go no further in making a claim.

The border control and compliance section of DIMIA conducted the initial interview. The purpose of the interview was to identify the person who had arrived and to gather intelligence on the route of the journey taken to reach Australia and the assistance provided along the way, particularly by smugglers. In addition, the interview sought to gather information to determine whether the person had a prima facie case for engaging Australia's protection obligations.

From reading many of the case studies, a lot depended on the first interview. Especially important were the magic words, 'I have come to Australia to seek refugee status under the Refugee Convention.'

Apart from the 'magic words', what was said at the initial interview had an ultimate bearing on the credibility of the story, the length of processing and the length of time the asylum seeker would stay in a detention centre. If the asylum seeker exhausted all legal avenues, often taking more than a year of processing time, the options were for the person to return to his country of origin or to seek refuge in an alternative country. If neither of these options were available then the asylum seeker would remain in the detention centre indefinitely.

Under a likely fear of interrogation and recently having survived an often-perilous voyage by sea, not to mention all the other types of trauma they would have experienced, it is not unreasonable for asylum seekers to inadvertently omit facts of significance and to say things to their disadvantage. Statements that were presented at the first interview and were not supported or repeated at subsequent interviews made it difficult for the case officer to view the applicant's story in a credible light. And it was similar with statements not made at the first interview but in the second and third interviews. A refusal by the case officer after the third interview meant that the applicant had to appeal to the Refugee Review Tribunal— often unnecessary in terms of legal costs and the extra trauma for the detainee.

Dr Al Jabiri, a lawyer with the Human Rights and Migration Services, drew attention to the concerns expressed by the Federal Court that the tribunal placed too much reliance on inconsistencies stemming from the initial interview:

[B]efore departing from the present case I would make certain observations about the increasing reliance by the RRT on prior inconsistent statements as a reason for rejecting an applicant's claim. As has been observed on numerous occasions the RRT should approach such statements with caution, make due allowances for linguistic, cultural and other difficulties confronting applicants for refugee status who are required to pursue their claims in an alien environment that they are likely to perceive as hostile' (Merkel in the Full Court Case of Al Shamry on 24 July 2001 at paragraph 63).

Dr Al Jabiri, in a letter to the presiding member of the Refugee Review Tribunal, described how social trauma in the applicant's home country could influence their responses:

The Tribunal, we submit, must always be mindful of the social conditions of the applicant's home country and how this can affect their responses to Australian persons of authority when the asylum seeker is first confronted with such persons on their arrival in Australia. It constitutes, we suggest, a powerful reason for discounting what is said at the first interview.

Our experience has been particularly with asylum seekers from Syria, Iraq, Iran and Afghanistan. There is clear evidence from the applicants themselves as well as for the volume of country information reports that all of these countries are, in essence, repressive police states, with as one noted observer has said 'regular arbitrary searches, arrests, detentions, torture, and periodic purges at a senior level.'

. . . There is a natural tendency therefore to maintain the same fearful suspicions when they come before an Australian interrogator about whom they know nothing at that early stage. They still regard themselves as being in what Merkel described as an 'alien and hostile environment'.

Furthermore many of our detainee clients report they have been misinformed about their status and their situation in Australia by many others along the way, including the smugglers who assisted them in other countries, by fellow detainees who arrived earlier, and at times even by the interpreters supplied for those initial interviews.

They also fear that what they say can or will be leaked back to the security authorities in their embassies or other posts in Australia and thereby put their families still in their home country at risk of harassment. Their fears in some instances may be justified, DIMA's claims of the sanctity of their privacy notwithstanding.

Thus, no matter what is said on forms translated to them, they are often misguidedly cautious and guarded in what they reveal about themselves. It is not until they speak with an adviser some months later as part of the process of applying for their protection visa that they develop a much better appreciation of what is expected of them and the very different official climate prevailing in Australia. Then they become more forthcoming (Jabiri 2000).

In his book, *Borderline*, Peter Mares also exposed ways in which asylum seekers were deprived of legal rights.

Section 193 of the Act effectively removes any obligation on an officer of the Commonwealth to inform a detainee of his or her legal rights, if that detainee has not successfully cleared immigration. Boat people seeking asylum fall into this category and since late 1994 it has become routine departmental practice not to advise them of their right to see a lawyer or of their right to apply for refugee status.

Mary Crock, a solicitor and legal academic, who had practised and written extensively in the fields of immigration and refugee law, spoke of Australia's obligation to identify real refugees. On Radio National (12 February 2001) she said to Geraldine Doogue, 'It shouldn't be a matter of trickery whether you identify a real refugee or not. There should be at least sufficient information given to the asylum seeker on arrival, if not legal advice, about the refugee processing system.'

Dr Amir, who had been in the Woomera detention centre for 11 months, described the first interview from a detainee's perspective:

> One of the most important stages of processing an applicant's claim is the initial interview which usually takes place four to seven days after arrival in Australia. The applicants are never told exactly how to behave and what to say to the DIMIA representative who interviews them. Most people leave their villages or towns for the first time in their lives, often from a poor and ravaged part of their land, to a developed and modern, Western-style country. The traumas and fears they experience in their own country resurface in a detention environment with harsh, prison-like conditions. They don't know that the chances of their cases being accepted depend mostly on the first interview, and as a result many applicants don't tell all the facts of their stories or cases during that interview. Later, they mix with other previously detained asylum seekers and get advice to tell all the details about their cases during the second and third interviews. When they try to do that they have a greater chance of being refused since the case officer will generally consider these additions or changes in details as new information, not consistent with the first interview, or fabrication.

As described earlier about 200 asylum seekers had been screened out after their first interview. Many were Iranians—an extra factor which did not count in their favour. They had been put into a separate compound to ponder their ultimate fate—no-one had informed them why but it soon became obvious. They had been able to restart the process with the help of the magic words: 'I have come to Australia to seek refugee status under the Refugee Convention.' This had meant the applicants could have the required three interviews for an assessment by their case officer. These delays would not have been necessary if proper legal advice had been given before the first interview. How long they would have languished there without resorting to a peaceful protest and receiving proper advice from a lawyer was anyone's guess.

Other asylum seekers were less fortunate—even after six months some had not proceeded beyond the first interview. In one case, an Iranian had waited nearly eight months for his second interview—all without any legal representation or reason given by DIMIA for the delay. Eventually, after his second and third interviews, his case officer refused a protection visa. This had been too much for him—he tried to hang himself and would have succeeded were it not for the watchful eye of a security officer. His case went to the Refugee Review Tribunal (RRT) and he was accepted, as a refugee, after 11 months at Woomera.

The initial interview could cause some further problems. Discrepancies arose because of omitting something considered relevant at a subsequent interview. Other discrepancies occurred with details of dates, locations and events. A lot of weight was given to the credibility of the applicant's stories and any discrepancy could mean rejection by the case officer—adding further delay to an eventual outcome. An appointed lawyer, if the detainee were able to afford one, could help to clarify the applicant's story, accounting for any discrepancies and emphasising the dangers of returning to the applicant's country.

In the meantime, the applicant became more despondent and more depressed. The psychologists and medical officers were overwhelmed with suicidal cases. That no-one had taken their life was a miracle as well as a tribute to those caring for them.

Migration agents, appointed by DIMIA to assist the applicants in their cases, rarely gave helpful advice. Their function appeared to be mainly as a recorder. Mary Lindsay, a registered migration agent with 15 years' experience, was expected to process up to four applications a day—an unrealistic task if it were to be done properly. There were many complaints also with interpreters who, despite their training, lacked the professional capacity to translate the full meaning of what was said.

There was another problem that caused frustration and anger. It mostly concerned the Afghanis who believed they had a genuine case—all claimed persecution by the Taliban. Imagine how they felt after being rejected while those who had been living in Pakistan for one or more years obtained a temporary protection visa. Because of this, four Afghanis started a riot on 8 June 2001. For eight hours, they and others in the main compound went on a rampage breaking windows and destroying computers and music instruments.

I asked one who came from Kabul how he could tell that some of those who claimed to have come from Afghanistan had actually come from Pakistan, even though they would have lived in Afghanistan some time in the past. 'Oh, it's easy, after ten minutes of talking with them we know,' he replied. 'We know who are the genuine Afghanis by the way they speak. More than 50 per cent have lived in Pakistan. Many have already been released.'

As far as I was concerned I was happy for anyone to leave Woomera but this posed a lot of questions. Why were the DIMIA-appointed linguistic experts not picking this up? If they were, why was it not important? Why was DIMIA apparently being soft with some and not with others? Was the processing system itself fraught with inconsistencies?

There had been cases of Afghanis claiming to be illiterate and coming from simple farming backgrounds. On release it had been discovered that they could communicate well in English. When they were asked where they had learned their English they responded, 'At the Woomera detention centre.' On being asked by the DIMIA Manager, David Frenchman, whether this was possible, I replied, 'No, I don't think so.' One of the Afghani detainees, rejected by RRT, believed that these 'illiterate' Pushtuns were supporters of the Taliban.

With the defeat of the Taliban in Afghanistan all the remaining Afghanis were likely to be sent back as soon as arrangements could be made.

In another situation a number of Sabian Mandeans had been rejected while others had been accepted. One family of four actually received their TPVs in just over two months. Country information supported the claims that Sabian Mandeans could suffer discrimination. One of them explained to me why his case was refused: 'The case officer did not believe I suffered mistreatment that amounted to persecution.' This person had been in the centre for more than eight months and had little chance of being released with the refusal of his appeal to the Refugee Review Tribunal. The same story repeated itself for some 60 Sabian Mandeans—most had been at the detention centre for more than nine months.

Were the differences in outcome for Sabian Mandeans and others a reflection of the differences in perception of the level of persecution by case officers? Or were there other reasons? One case officer, no doubt compassionate, had accepted most cases including those from Iran. Another case officer had rejected nearly all of his cases. There were lucky outcomes for some and an agonising wait for others.

Coming from Iraq was a plus in terms of persecution, as shown with the group of some 50 Assyrian Christians who were able to bring stronger evidence, along with Country Information Services reports, of being persecuted. All were granted temporary protection visas.

In addition to the above, there were mistakes made by case officers. Some of these mistakes would be laughable if they had not caused so much anguish for the applicants. A case officer who was not well organised to handle a number of cases could quite easily get the loose notes mixed up. In one situation the name of the applicant had been attached to a completely different case story. In another, the story of one applicant was applied to two other applicants. The migration agent, as the legal representative of the applicant, should have picked up these mistakes. Unfortunately, there was no way the applicant could get back to the case officer once the primary decision had been made. The applicant had to write a letter to the Refugee Review Tribunal to explain what had happened and that usually took a further two to three months to resolve. In a third situation, two cases were shelved for three months when the case officer left the job with no advice to the new case officer about outstanding cases.

In a classic 'cut and paste' job Mohammed, an Iraqi, wrote a letter to his RRT member:

I fled Iraq fearing for my safety and came to Australia seeking asylum like most of the oppressed and persecuted people. I respect the Australian rules of law and I accept to be treated fairly as an asylum seeker in accordance with those rules. I thought that once I am in Australia I should feel safe and reassured that I would not find the same injustice and corruption that I experienced in my own country.

The way my visa application was processed was far from being fair and professional and this creates in me a feeling of mistrust and a doubt in the credibility of the Australian systems. In the worst conditions of Woomera detention centre, I have been waiting for about nine months for a decision for my protection visa application. That decision finally arrived but based on incorrect and untrue information, or information not related to my case.

To start with, if we look at the first page, in the introduction the decision maker states that the smuggler took my Iraqi passport and gave me a Moroccan passport for my travel to Indonesia; I don't know where he got this information from, because I have never said in my interview anything like that. Noting also that he wrote that I left Iraq on 1/7/2000 and then later, on two occasions, stated that I left Iraq once on 11/7/2000 and the next time on 17/7/2000! What can we conclude from these errors? But it doesn't end here:

In item 2, the issue of linguistic expert's opinion that my dialect was a typical local dialect spoken by Palestinians residing in Kuwait etc . . . Obviously the interview tapes he is talking about belong to a different applicant because I can assure you that I am a genuine Iraqi of an Iraqi father, and I have provided relevant ID documents that support my claim. My documents and the interview tapes are still in the possession of the case officer. It is important to know that the interpreter who was present at the interview was not an Iraqi national, and on a few occasions she told me that she was finding it hard to understand my Iraqi accent so I had to answer some questions using the classic Arabic language which is the official language of all Arab countries spoken on radio and TV. Noting that the accent by the Palestinians is more or less closer to the classical language. However I am not a Palestinian and I have never been to Kuwait.

I need to draw your attention to the fact that on the day I was given the decision letter, another Iraqi detainee in the camp also received his decision letter, and to our surprise (or should I say shock) most of the reasons for rejection given to both of us are similar at least in regard to the linguistic test. I am almost convinced that this decision maker has deliberately abused his position and filled these letters (using the cut and paste method) with incorrect and negative information just to pass his rejection to our applications.

The decision maker claims in the decision record that I told a story during the interview about a raid by the regime forces against a group of people who were having a religious meeting in Diwaniya and he does not believe how I could escape from that raid. Your Honour, the fact is I have never been to Diwaniya and I have never mentioned anything during any of my interviews about me being involved with a religious group and being raided by the regime forces during our meeting! He also claims that I stated that my two brothers, Ahmad and Kazim, were detained by the regime forces and I know nothing about their whereabouts. My answer to that is the fact that I have no brother called Kazim but I have one 9 years old brother called Ahmad and the regime forces never detained him. This story obviously must have been told by another applicant and has nothing to do with my case or me.

The DIMIA officer has apparently mixed up many application papers together and he could not tell anymore which paper belonged to which applicant. So, do I have to bear the consequences of his negligence and irresponsibility? At school they teach us to revise our homework and check whether there is still any mistake. This is not school homework, it is a vital issue concerning people's fate. Building a decision like that on false information means that the person has no sense of responsibility and would only like to see people suffer pretending that he is doing his job!

Finally I would like to express my astonishment toward a statement made by the decision maker on the top of the last page of the decision record in which he stated: 'I have carefully considered the totality of the applicant's claims and relevant country information . . .' If this person after all the clear errors found in his record, claims to be careful, I wonder what disaster he might create when not being careful.

I have faith in your tribunal and I am certain that you are going to make the correct decision regarding my appeal, after looking at all the facts.

Respectfully yours
Mohammed

Fortunately, the RRT members were more careful and recognised the mistakes made by case officers. Some of the mistakes were so obvious that there was no need to call a hearing. The ACM-appointed interpreters generally regarded the RRT members as open-minded and knowledgeable about up-to-date country information and that usually worked to the advantage of the applicant.

From talking to many detainees about their cases, to lawyers, to interpreters on site and to other officers, it became apparent that the processing system was flawed and caused unnecessary and lengthy delays. The reasons were:

- the nature of the initial interview: it was short, calculating and without any legal advice or representation;
- the difficulties in establishing credibility following the initial interview;
- the perfunctory nature of duties performed by the migration agents;

- the arbitrary and inconsistent nature of the decision-making process and the potential for mistakes made by the case officer;
- the lack of access to independent lawyers at any stage of the processing system;
- the decision made by only one member of the Refugee Review Tribunal.

The problems with the interpreters were especially evident with the Sabian Mandeans who came from Iran. They had suffered discrimination and persecution under the Islam Shiite regime. Their Shiite Muslim interpreter at the detention centre, however, was, it was felt, often frustrated when hearing these stories and reluctant to interpret anything that put the Shiite religion in a bad light. It was common knowledge that the Shiite Muslims usually considered Sabian Mandeans as infidels: that is, unclean and unfaithful people. Consequently, it was difficult to see how any Sabian Mandean asylum seeker could be treated objectively by a Shiite Muslim interpreter.

For the Hazara detainees from Afghanistan there were no interpreters who spoke Hazaragi to help them through the process. Even the linguistic experts who analysed the language which people used during the interviews were not familiar enough with the Hazaragi words, and in any case, had left Afghanistan many years earlier. According to Hassan, a Hazara and delegate for the Afghanis, with whom I spoke after his release, about two-thirds of the Hazara people had had their applications rejected on the basis of language. They had been told that they were Pakistani or Iranian.

All of these difficulties in processing cases highlighted a significant 'grey area' that allowed some asylum seekers to be released when technically they did not fit the 1951 Refugee Convention and others who regarded themselves as genuine but having to appeal against adverse decisions. There were more questions that needed answering: Was the processing system unworkable and, therefore, adding to the trauma of detainees? Was the Howard Government aware of this? If so, why was it persisting with it? Was it to keep up appearances of a hardline and punitive approach to deter others from coming?

From December 2001, in response to the legal inadequacies, up to 50 Australian lawyers and a Queen's Counsel provided free legal advice to detainees at the Woomera detention centre. The lawyers, with the help of church and human-services groups, operated a Woomera lawyers' group.

Adelaide-based lawyer, Jeremy Moore, said that they wanted to provide free services to the detainees 'whose legal rights have been trampled over'. After hearing about the lengthy delays in the processing of cases, he and Paul Boylan, also a lawyer, decided to help out. Dr Amir recounts his own involvement with the *pro bono* team.

About three months before my release, I met with Paul Boylan, a tough lawyer. He listened to my story and was outraged about the delay in my case. Then Jeremy Moore came to see me as well as other detainees to see what could be done to help us. However, we were faced with a dilemma. Since we were under the auspices of DIMIA and ACM we succumbed to their threats and demands not to see Jeremy; otherwise our cases would be jeopardised.

After my release on 19 December 2000, I met Jeremy Moore by chance in Victoria Square in Adelaide. It was the starting point of going back to the Woomera detention centre and working with the lawyers as an interpreter. I could see that my presence brought hope for people there.

In October 2001 we received financial support from various humanitarian organisations, which allowed the group to lease a house in Woomera town named Woomera Legal Outpost. This is now a base for members of the group who want to stay for any length of time to help detainees in their cases. Everyone is determined to do as much as possible.

The Woomera Legal Outpost in Woomera town

Some of the detainees at Woomera had now been there for about two years. One of them, an Iraqi, said: 'How could they, the Australian Government, be so cruel to us? If they don't want us, let them say sooner, not keep us waiting in such a state of misery. The conditions are not good but we can survive here for three months if we know there will be a definite answer, one way or the other.'

One of the biggest surprises expressed by detainees was to realise that the Australian Government appeared, in many respects, similar to the regime from which they had escaped.

In the middle of January 2002 about 950 detainees remained at the Woomera detention centre; they had been there more than five months and a few had passed their second year. It was time to grant a pardon—an amnesty—to those who had dared to come 'illegally' to our shores, braving our mandatory detention environment and legal system. It was time to release everyone under a reporting system and to work through the cases more thoroughly to arrive at the best outcome. It was time to find an alternative for the policy of mandatory detention.

The November and December 2001 riots had brought months of simmering tension to a head. Perceived inequities in the processing system gave rise to frustration, desperation and pent-up anger—erupting into uncontrollable acts of destruction. Following the rioting and burning episodes, the detainees adopted a new strategy to draw attention to their plight—hunger strikes and lip-sewing. Emotions ran high on both sides of the fence. A nation became divided. More questions were asked.

In Canberra, the Howard Government had pushed its hardline policies, supported by myths about asylum seekers and by a deep-seated fear in the Australia psyche that hordes of unwanted aliens were pressing in on us. The Labor Party was quiet—it was a bi-partisan approach—it was politically unwise to rock the boat. There was no debate at the major party political level; there was no alternative to mandatory detention—and the suffering and riots continued.

Even the Governor-General, Dr Peter Hollingworth, was quiet as Phillip Adams wrote in *The Weekend Australian* (1–2 December 2001):

> I've been waiting for him to say something, say something, say anything, on the moral, ethical, and yes, spiritual issues raised by this, the most profound and divisive crisis we've faced in decades.

In an earlier article entitled 'Beware: bigotry is back', Phillip Adams had defined the reasons for the existence of the detention centres: 'to warn off the asylum seekers by replacing the symbolism of the Olympic torch with the sweep of the searchlight; and to play to Australia's racial paranoia, to the One Nation factor as the election drums are beating' (*The Weekend Australian* 1–2 September 2001).

A BETTER WAY?

In Australia we have persisted with mandatory detention that breaches a number of international conventions which had provisions for treating people with dignity and respect. In regard to the Refugee Convention itself, people should not be subject to punitive measures and should be allowed to move around freely in the country in which they have sought asylum.

When I finished my contract at the beginning of September 2001 some 460 mainly Afghani asylum seekers were cooped up on a Norwegian cargo ship, the *Tampa*, waiting for the Australian Government to make a decision where they could land. The president of the Uniting Church, James Haire, led a delegation of the heads of churches to Canberra on 30 August 2001 and called for the Government to allow the asylum seekers to land on Christmas Island. The Government hardened its stance though, and refused to let them land on Australian territory; instead, they took them to Nauru. The United Nations Human Rights Commissioner, Mary Robinson, denounced Australia for its lack of compassion. The 'fortress mentality' adopted by the Government was similar to that adopted by some European governments.

The United Nations High Commissioner for Refugees, Ruud Lubbers, laid the blame partly on Western governments for the large numbers of people moving around the world: 'You cannot complain if you are not prepared to give money needed for solutions in the regions where the refugees come from,' he said in a BBC interview.

Ruud Lubbers also attacked politicians who demonised asylum

seekers. In *The Australian* (20 June 2001) he described what was happening in some countries, including Australia:

> Asylum seekers have become a campaign issue in various recent and uncompromising election battles, with Governments and Opposition parties vying to appear toughest on the 'bogus' asylum seekers 'flooding' into their countries. In some nations—Australia, Austria, Denmark, Italy, and Britain, for example—individual politicians and media appear at times to be deliberately inflating the issue. Statistics are frequently manipulated, facts are taken out of context, and the character of asylum seekers as a group is often distorted in order to present them as a terrible threat—a threat their detractors can then pledge to crush.
>
> Asylum seekers make a perfect target for people who want to invoke the age-old prejudice against foreigners. Asylum seekers cannot answer back. Illegal, bogus, flood, fraudulent, criminal, scrounger, trafficking—all these words are commonly paired with the term 'asylum seeker'. Such words drip into the public consciousness until they become self-fulfilling—the public opinion they help shape stimulates the formulation of increasingly restrictive and harsher policies.

Were there any alternatives to mandatory detention? If there were, should not we consider them? A number of individuals and organisations have.

The National Council of Churches and Hotham Mission ran a forum on Australia's treatment of asylum seekers on 12 April 2001. The forum was attended by over 50 organisations. Among its recommendations, the forum called upon the Australian Government to cease undermining its own living-in-harmony program through the vilification of asylum seekers and to adopt a less xenophobic and more tolerant approach to its coverage of asylum seekers and refugees. The forum also recommended that detention should be limited to health, security and identity checks for unauthorised arrivals for a maximum of two months. All children and families should be released from detention as quickly as possible. Unaccompanied minors should be released into the care of child-protection agencies.

In a similar way, Amnesty International also called on the Federal Government to consider alternatives to mandatory detention.

Justice for Asylum Seekers, a Victoria-based coalition representing 34 groups, proposed an alternative detention model that included:

- more humane treatment of people on arrival and when they are in detention, including ensuring that they understand the process and their rights, and have access to appropriate independent health and legal professionals;
- greater flexibility in the consideration of a person's individual circumstances when deciding on their status;
- equity of treatment between those who are detained and those who are not; around 85 per cent of detainees are eventually cleared by immigration, yet in detention they are treated as if they are 'guilty' until proven 'innocent';
- reducing the time every individual spends in detention, including maximum time limits, thereby making considerable savings and allowing people to live in the community where most eventually settle;
- through these and other steps, bringing the detention regime into line with Australia's international-treaty obligations, and addressing the criticisms of the United Nations Human Rights Committee.

(Caroline Green, 15 December 2001, website: www.onlineopinion.com.au)

In New South Wales, Rural Australians for Refugees, a group formed during the election campaign and which attracted 400 people to its first meeting at Moss Vale, set out a ten-point plan asking the Government to:

- receive all asylum seekers in accordance with Australia's obligations under the 1951 United Nations Convention on

Refugees of which Australia was a signatory. After being assessed, asylum seekers would either be accepted as genuine refugees or deported, according to long-established criteria;

- abolish existing holding centres in Nauru and Papua New Guinea and abandon any further plans to pay our poorer Pacific neighbours to take refugees for processing;

- stop military intervention against boat people. Using Australia's military against victims of oppression is totally inappropriate;

- abolish the Temporary Protection Visas (TPVs), which were introduced specifically for asylum seekers, who mainly arrive by boat. These visas deny people access to crucial services such as English lessons, and work and housing assistance, which are available to other refugees. Recent changes to the TPV mean that people can never obtain permanent residency and will never obtain permanent residency and will never be allowed to reunite with their immediate family, such as a wife and children;

- close all detention centres in their present form. Asylum seekers should be held in detention only to establish their current identity and for criminal clearance, along the lines of the Swedish model. As in Sweden, children should only be held in detention for a maximum of six days;

- take any detention facilities out of the hands of private enterprise. Such facilities should be publicly accountable and open to scrutiny, rather than be left to the mercy of the profit motive;

- recognise that there is an international humanitarian crisis of huge proportions that Australia cannot ignore, and which involves the mass migration of refugees and displaced people. Australia should lead an international search for cooperative solutions and support a worldwide increase in aid for refugees;

- actively work with Indonesia and other countries to stop the dangerous and criminal activities of 'people smugglers'. At the same time, find a safer and more humane way to bring asylum seekers to Australia for processing;

- promote the establishment of an international conference to review international conventions and revise current inadequate procedures for resettlement of refugees;
- increase Australia's refugee intake by recognising how small our current quota of 12,000 refugees per year is, and doubling the quota to 24,000 per year.

(Unity No. 279, 23 November 2001)

The Refugee Council of Australia also proposed alternatives including limited detention for no more than three months.

In an editorial, *The Australian* (20 December 2001) described the Woomera riot in December as exposing a flawed system:

At the core of the asylum seekers' desperation is the frustrating cascading appeals process. It is unnecessarily complicated and lengthy, and simply feeds into the cycle of despondency. The Federal Government must devise a new policy towards asylum seekers that moves away from mandatory detention and deals with claims more fairly, more speedily and with genuine decency.

There are a number of examples from other countries for alternative ways to process asylum seekers; one of these is the Swedish model. Grant Mitchell, who had spent two years working for the Swedish Migration Board, including one year at the Carlslund detention centre, wrote a paper, 'Asylum seekers in Sweden', in which he described an integrated approach to reception, detention, determination, integration and return. He wrote:

Sweden has been successful in building a functioning reception process that allows for a just and humane treatment of asylum seekers while they await their decision, addresses national security concerns and effectively removes failed refugee-claimants. Sweden has also been successful in quickly integrating resettled refugees into society.

According to Mitchell, all asylum seekers spent at least two weeks in the Carlslund Refugee Reception Centre, which included a detention centre. The maximum a person could be kept in detention was two months. After completing the initial application, the asylum seeker usually moved to a regional refugee centre to await the outcome of the application process. During this time the asylum seeker was free to come and go but had to report to the central office at least monthly.

New Zealand completed the processing of 130 refugees from the *Tampa* by the end of January 2002, at a cost of A$1.6 million. The processing was carried out in a resettlement centre without resorting to razor wire.

In Canada, detention of asylum seekers was the exception rather than the rule, and limited to specific cases such as persons who could be a danger to the public or likely to abscond or work without a work permit. The Canadians had worked out a way to be more flexible, to focus on the spirit of the Refugee Convention, rather than the letter of the law.

It was a similar story with the United States of America.

For Australia, the Pacific solution that diverted asylum seekers to remote islands, along with the mandatory detention system, would cost hundreds of millions of dollars. Could some of that money be used to improve the refugee process, to help them in resettlement and to allow them to add value to our way of life?

Mark Raper, Director of Uniya, the Jesuit Social Justice Centre, cited a number of alternatives to mandatory detention:

These non-custodial measures include the supervised release of children and young adults to community services; the supervised release to non-government organisation; release on bail to an individual citizen; release with restrictions on place of residence and reporting requirements; accommodation in open centres to which the asylum seeker returns each evening.

(Eureka Street, April 2002)

Could Australians follow the lead from other countries to explore alternatives and develop its own model? Or were we too fearful to move and perhaps too inflexible to see beyond the myths, half-truths and simplistic rhetoric?

In 50 years' time a historian will add another shameful page to Australia's history. Enlightened people will ask how it could have happened. The world came to our doorstep and as a nation we retreated into fear and darkness. Nelson Mandela's inaugural speech in 1994 (Pretoria, South Africa) talked about liberating ourselves from our fears and liberating others. We did not choose that way.

As an island we are protected from the poverty of Third World countries, the refugee camps, the squalor of living conditions, life's deprivation and the despair of millions. A few—only a few thousand—did make it to our shores. They were branded and dealt with 'appropriately'. From a national perspective, an opportunity to show compassion was squandered. There was no alternative, according to the Howard Government, but to imprison and punish them so others would think twice about coming to our sacred land. For those who came across the Timor Sea we were not sharing our boundless plains.

In the same vein I saw another side at Woomera; a side you could discover only on sharing some time with the people who desperately wanted a new life. To give an asylum seeker a visa is to give an opportunity to experience the freedom we take for granted. The razor wire at Woomera was a symbolic reminder of this, of what they have come from and what they need now in Australia. Some will be fortunate and move beyond the razor wire; others will not. Dr Amir, a microbiologist from Iraq, spent 11 months at Woomera and described it this way: 'They came to Australia to find relief and found a different sorrow.'

In another way, the asylum seekers have been good for Australia—it has brought the world to our doorstep. If it hadn't happened now it would have happened later. People have responded in different ways; people have voiced their opinions from different perspectives and people have become aware of other countries less fortunate than our own. As Nelson Mandela wrote in the *Long Walk to Freedom*, 'For to be free is not merely to cast off one's chains, but to live in a way that respects and enhances the freedom of others.' To cast off our Australian chains—our fears, our entrenched attitudes and our restricting legalism—would be the first step in offering dignity and self-respect to others.

BEHIND AND BEYOND THE WIRE

From September 2001 to April 2002 events moved rapidly, inside and outside the Woomera detention centre, to raise more hackles and provoke more questions concerning asylum seekers.

Soon after the September 11 terrorist attacks in the United States, the Defence Minister, Peter Reith, said that the unauthorised arrival of boats on Australian territory could be 'a pipeline for terrorists' to come in and use Australia as a staging post for terrorist activities.

In September also, a new surveillance to deter boat people arriving in north-western Australia swung into operation with the committal of five navy warships and four *P-3 Orion* aircraft, at an estimated cost of A$3 million a day. Combined with the Pacific solution to divert boat people to Pacific islands it effectively meant that there would be no more asylum seekers landing in Australia by boat. The new mission for the Defence Forces was known as Operation Relex. Later, ABC *Four Corners* gave a graphic account of the suffering and anguish when the Navy frigate *Warramunga* escorted about 230 asylum seekers from Ashmore Reef to the island of Roti, close to West Timor. To avoid panic, it was done under the pretence of going to Australia (ABC *Four Corners*, 15 April 2002).

In late September, there was a stand-off on HMAS *Manoora* when 217 Iraqis and Palestinians refused to disembark from the Australian navy ship anchored off Nauru, one of the Pacific islands that had responded to Australia's inducements to provide a haven for asylum seekers while being processed. The boat people on the

HMAS *Manoora* feared that they would be left on the tiny Pacific island indefinitely. After a few days, the Australian authorities allayed their fears and they disembarked.

On 19 October, 353 people drowned with only 44 being rescued when an overcrowded Indonesian boat, known as SIEV X, sank on its way to Christmas Island. It was the single worst disaster for asylum seekers coming to Australia. Later questions were asked of the Australian Navy as to their knowledge of the boat in distress and, if they were aware of the boat's plight, why was anything not done about it, especially if the boat was in international waters when it went down.

In late October, the Government released a video purporting to show parents throwing their children overboard in an effort to intimidate the Government. Later, conveniently after the Federal election, this claim was proved to be false.

In November, the Human Rights Commissioner announced that there would be a national inquiry into children in immigration detention. It would cover the international human rights obligations with respect to issues relating to health, education, culture, guardianship, security practices and conditions under which children were detained.

Inside the Woomera centre, a new crisis followed the December riots. In the middle of January, at the same time as I took up a six-month contract with Torrens Valley TAFE as coordinator of English courses for migrants, 370 Afghani detainees went on a hunger strike with 35 of them sewing their lips together. One was Alamdar, whose uncle had plunged into the razor wire on 26 January.

Six were hospitalised before the hunger strike ended. Members of a Federal Government advisory body, the Immigration Detention Advisory Group, headed by former chief of Australia's air staff, Ray Funnell, succeeded in bringing to an end the 16-day hunger strike after a commitment was given to resume the processing of Afghani visa applications.

Frank Brennan, a lawyer and social justice campaigner, who visited the centre at the time of the hunger strike, said:

> The people here have some legitimate concerns. They are mystified that members of the Australian public would be critical of them when they get to a stage of hunger-striking and stitching lips.

From the beginning of October to the start of the hunger strike on 15 January only a few detainees had been released in contrast to some 30 a week before September 11. The Afghanis discussed their options with the Iraqis and the Iranians. Some wanted to escape and someone suggested cutting the hydraulic lead to the front gate. Hassan Varasi, the Afghani delegate, persuaded them that a peaceful protest would be better. Setting fire to buildings had not worked, escaping into the Australian desert would be futile and any type of violence had really turned against them.

A hunger strike was the best option although some had reservations since the Iranians had just been on hunger strike for eight days and the Afghanis on a separate occasion for six days, all with no response. With everyone gathered to discuss the options Hassan said, 'We should try again, people outside are more supportive.'

'We need to talk to someone on the outside if it is going to work,' someone replied.

Hassan said, 'I will do it. I will accept the risk of this.'

On the third day of the hunger strike Hassan contacted *The Australian* and the next day there was just a small item. Then David Frenchman, head of the Department of Immigration Multicultural and Indigenous Affairs (DIMIA) at the Woomera centre, prohibited the use of all phones. Hassan had asked to use a phone.

'If you stop self-harming, I will think about this,' David Frenchman was reported as saying.

Shortly after, about twelve detainees started climbing the razor wire fence.

'Stop them,' David Frenchman had ordered.

'I will stop them if you give me a phone,' Hassan had replied.

'I will talk to the ACM manager,' David Frenchman had said.

A short time after, Hassan had been able to use the phone again to talk to someone in the ABC for five minutes. After that, he had phoned every day during the hunger strike and talked for as long as he liked.

On the seventh day of the hunger strike the Immigration Detention Advisory Group (IDAG) met the delegates. With advice from the lawyer, Jeremy Moore and others, the Afghanis presented their demands to the IDAG:

> We Afghani protestors, who have entered the seventh day of hunger strike at Woomera detention centre, would like to welcome the Immigration Advisory Committee Group, who have been appointed

ABOVE: Hunger strikers sheltering under bedding around the internal perimeter fence of the Main Compound.

Photographs obtained from the Human Rights and Equal Opportunity Commission's National Inquiry into Children in Immigration Detention: reproduced from website http://www.humanrights.gov.au/index.html

OPPOSITE PAGE: Woomera breakout (Easter 2002)

Photo by Peter Mathew

by the Department of Immigration, Multicultural and Indigenous Affairs to assess the situation surrounding our latest protest and hunger strike.

We would like to present our demands as follows:

Our long existence in a non-healthy environment such as Woomera prison has traumatised all of us psychologically. When we are free from this place, we will be emancipated from madness and illness. Therefore, we cannot tolerate staying any longer in this fearful prison beyond the razor wires.

From our point of view, the current political situation in Afghanistan and the composition of the interim government is only a superficial change and a change of pawns. We believe there has not been any fundamental change in our country. The major cities and provinces are still in the hands of the warlords and there are still wars over language, race and tribal differences in Afghanistan. Lack of security, mass destruction and the planting of 70 per cent of different kinds of landmines from around the world as well as the presence of armed people in Afghanistan are the factors which make it impossible for the Afghan refugees to return to their country. If they return they will be faced with death and persecution and then it will be again a massive tragedy.

Our hope and expectation of the Australian and international community will be for them to pay serious attention to the human rights of the protestors at Woomera detention centre, who have been struggling for their survival and their rights, which have been totally abused. Now we are entering the seventh day of the hunger strike with stitches on our lips, under the hot sun. This represents the human tragedy in the heart of Australia. We are calling upon you to take an urgent decision about our faith and freedom as soon as possible. To send delegations and hold negotiations with no thought of practical action would not heal our trauma at all. We are fed up with today and tomorrow's promises. We want clear answers to our calls for freedom. We will continue to our protest until our death. We prefer death to captivity in this fearful prison.

IDAG responded positively to their demands and suggested a meeting in three days' time when they would come again. More discussions followed at this meeting but there was no agreement.

On day 15 of the hunger strike three members of IDAG, Ray Funnell, Paris Aristotle and Harry Minas, visited the Woomera centre. The discussions rolled on to day 16 when there was a breakthrough after several hours of talking with delegates. The Afghani detainees decided to end the hunger strike. There was an offer from IDAG to recommence the processing of claims.

A media statement put out by the Afghanis, through the Woomera lawyers' group, covered the promises made by IDAG to the Afghani people at the Woomera detention centre:

- Five Hazaraghi interpreters will be immediately provided to assist with the rapid and fair processing of Afghani refugee applications;
- Fast and fair processing of all applications for the Afghani people;
- Proper Hazaraghi interpreters and language experts for processing initial applications and appeals to the Refugee Review Tribunal (RRT) and Federal Court;
- Afghani people who have language objections from DIMIA in relation to their applications and have not responded in time to those objections, those objections will be cancelled;
- Afghani people who have completed their third interview and have not had a response for up to six months, those people will receive rapid answers, being yes or no. Other Afghani people who have been waiting for more than six months following the completion of their third interview will not be rejected in their applications;
- Afghani people who have had applications rejected and are waiting to go on to the RRT will go to the RRT as soon as possible;
- Afghani people who have been to the RRT hearing and have

Protesting against the detention of asylum seekers
(Easter 2002)
Photo by Peter Mathew

not had an answer now will be given an answer yes or no very quickly and that decision will be fair;

- Afghani people who have been accepted by the RRT and have been waiting more than 15 months for a Temporary Protection Visa (TPV) will receive a TPV;
- RRT rejection and appeal to the Federal Court have been taking a long time. IDAG promise to make that much quicker. People who are accepted by the Federal Court and referred back to the RRT will have their RRT hearing dealt with quickly and fairly;

IDAG agreed to talk with the Minister for Immigration to respond in a positive way to the use of s417 (*Migration Act*) special circumstances applications in order to allow Afghani people to apply for consideration of special circumstances on a case-by-case basis.

November and Mike compounds on fire at the Woomera
detention centre (December 2002).

Photo by Peter Mathew

The IDAG group also recommended that there should be an end
to the processing of asylum seekers at the Woomera centre and that
it should be used only as an emergency overflow facility.

Human Rights and Equal Opportunity Commission (HREOC)
also visited Woomera detention centre at this time and carried out
a five-day assessment as part of a national inquiry into children in
detention centres. The commission concluded that there were clear
breaches of the Convention on the Rights of the Child, to which
Australia was a signatory. The official statistics provided to
HREOC officers by ACM indicated the following incidents of
self-harm over a two-week period:

- lip sewing: five children (one 14-year-old sewed his lips
  twice);
- slashing: three children (the above child also slashed
  'freedom' into his forearm);

- ingesting of shampoo: two children;
- attempted hanging: one child;
- threats of self-harm: 13 children

This was a significant proportion of 236 children at the centre. The HREOC officers reported that 'Woomera centre was enveloped in a self-reinforcing miasma of despair and despera-tion, and there was a widespread sense of despair due to the length of time in detention and the concomitant uncertainty over status.' It was this uncertainty that asylum seekers had indicated was at the root cause of fire and property destruction in December and hunger strikes and incidents of self-harm in late January. (*Unity* No 286, 8 February 2002)

Public concern increased following the hunger strike. DIMIA responded with stepping up the processing and released many detainees, including all the unaccompanied minors, over the next few weeks. Still, families who had been there for more than a year remained.

In response, a new organisation, Australians for Just Refugee Programs, was launched on 20 February 2002 with its charter statement:

> We believe that Australia's policies towards refugees and asylum seekers should at all times reflect respect, decency and traditional Australian generosity to those in need while advancing Australia's international standing and national interests. We aim to achieve just and compassionate treatment of refugees, consistent with human rights standards which Australia has developed and endorsed.

The South Australians for Justice for Refugees was established shortly after, working in partnership with this national body, to:
- build an active coalition of groups and individuals to lobby governments in support of a just and humane response toward asylum seekers;

- develop understanding of and support for asylum seekers at a grassroots level;
- enlist public support from community and opinion leaders.

At about this time, the Woomera detention centre became a 'hot' topic in leading international newspapers. Journalists flew into Adelaide, eager to find out what was really happening at Woomera and to pick up first-hand accounts of refugee stories. One of them, Southeast Asia Bureau Chief, Richard Paddock, of the *Los Angeles Times*, rang me at work. He wanted to speak to one of the unaccompanied minors who had been released. I said that might be difficult but we might be able to speak to someone who had just turned 18. Essa, a former Afghani unaccompanied minor, was happy to tell his story so we met on a balmy, late summer's evening at the Hyatt Regency Adelaide. Essa explained that he had lost family members and that he had no knowledge about whether any of his family were still alive or how to go about finding about them. After Essa's account of his life in Afghanistan, his journey to Australia and what it had been like at the Woomera detention centre, Richard interviewed me and was keen to know anything about the Bakhtiaris—another story, he explained, for the *Los Angeles Times*.

In early March 2002 the secretary-general of Amnesty International, Irene Khan, spoke out against Australia's treatment of asylum seekers:

Australian politicians speak of the human rights of this country as 'second to none' but I am afraid the image of Australia is less of a carefree, sunburnt country sporting nation and more the image of *Tampa* and its human cargo, of riots and protests at Woomera, of Australian-funded detention centres on the Pacific Islands . . . It is all too easy to feed people's fears that the threat comes from abroad, to create a climate of suspicion, mistrust, xenophobia and racism . . . to confuse those fleeing terror with those who are suspected of causing terror. (*The Age*, Wednesday 6 March 2002)

Meanwhile Sadiq, the artist, had sent a letter on the worsening situation at Woomera. He was still awaiting the decision of the Federal Court and wrote:

Dear Mr Tom,

Woomera is an unstable centre since last two months. Everyday residents try to cut themselves and hang from fences, showing their upset life in the centre.

Last night about 17 Iraqi people in November [compound] dug the earth and made graves for themselves and their children. Because of the heavy weight of soil their condition was not good this afternoon. This is against the slow motion of visa process. The Minister's advisory committee who came to Woomera several times didn't help the people who are rejected by the Refugee Review Tribunal and the Federal Court. There is no hope to be accepted by the Minister for these people.

The Jeremy Moore lawyers group who work voluntary for rejected people didn't take my case, so I wrote to the Minister without the help of a lawyer but get no answer.

What is the new government's policy about asylum seekers? What do you think?

Sadiq

Later in March, it was announced that the captain of the *Tampa*, Arne Rinman, and his crew, would receive the prestigious United Nations High Commissioner for Refugees award for their bravery in rescuing the 433 boat people off Indonesia. The honour contrasts with Australia's 'contribution' in refusing to let the asylum seekers, rescued by the *Tampa*, land at Christmas Island.

Tom Long, a star of *Sea Change* and *The Dish*, and a member of *Actors for Refugees*, told why he was angry at the bipartisan policy on the *Tampa* and related issues:

I felt there was a big section of the community whose views weren't being heard. We want ordinary Australians to find out about the real issues. If we can do that, we believe there would be a change in attitudes, and ultimately in government policy. Australians should be treating the asylum seekers with empathy—as if it were their kids, their families in this situation. These people have already been traumatised by horrendous circumstances. We have to get the children and their families out of detention. We need to speed up applications, and if people must be detained, it should be for a minimal time. This doesn't mean throwing open the gates, but we are only processing a tiny percentage of the world's refugees—surely we can do this in a more humane manner . . . Politicians aren't going to lead on this issue—ordinary Australians need to get active. Ultimately, we must treat these refugees the way we want to be treated ourselves. It is a reflection on the health of our society. Even from a cold, economic rationalist point of view, the current policy is not viable. From a humane perspective, it can't and shouldn't continue. The message has to come from the people.

(*Oxfam Horizons* vol. 2 no. 1, February 2002)

In a similar vein Frank Brennan, lawyer and social justice advocate, said:

The blanket detention policy and the Pacific solution are morally reprehensible. But we live in a democracy where there is neither the prevailing public opinion nor the moral assessment of our lawmakers. Given that detention is an integral part of the Government's present policy, it is essential that the time delays, uncertainties, and psychological trauma exacerbated by the events of September 11 and the Federal election now be put behind us as quickly as possible. Because of those events, every inmate in Woomera (including the bona fide refugees) will have spent an additional five months in detention—five months of despairing isolation which drove people to sew their lips so that they might be heard. Surely it is time for government and the community to respond with a renewed commitment to a determination process that is 'fair', just, economical, informal and quick.

(*Eureka Street*, April 2002)

At the grassroots level in Australia there were those who did respond—it was heartening to see this in so many small but important ways. In Adelaide, some were members of charitable organisations such as St Vincent De Paul and the Salvation Army; some were service providers such as the Australian Refugee Association, the Department of Human Services, the Red Cross and STTARS (Survivors of Torture and Trauma Rehabilitation Service); some were from churches such as the Lutheran Church of Australia at Blair Athol; some were organisations such as the Soroptimist International of South Australia and the Sophia Refugee Support Group; some were concerned individuals like Franco, who protested in his own way against the hardline response of the Government and spent Christmas Day in jail; some were families who welcomed them into their homes and some were foster parents for the unaccompanied minors.

In addition, there were monthly picnics to welcome refugees and forums and meetings to inform people about detention issues and to assist in shifting public opinion. Dr Amir from Iraq, Shahin from Iran and Hassan from Afghanistan were in constant demand as speakers. People wanted to have a better insight and understanding to the one portrayed by the media or the Government.

In South Australia, some high schools were also becoming involved by inviting speakers, especially those newly released, to come and talk about their experiences. 'Australia IS Refugees' was the title of a school project for the primary Years Six and Seven and for the high school; it was an Australian-wide project based on telling refugee stories.

On 2 March, five Adelaide bands played at the Governor Hindmarsh Hotel to raise money for the Australian Refugee

Association. At the foot of their flyer it stated: 'It's not about whether you agree or disagree—it's about human rights.' A conference for teachers, 'Society and Environment', held in April, included a keynote address on refugee issues by Yasmine Ahmed, a member of the Woomera lawyers group. People responded in many positive ways to help and, for those still in detention centres, they could write and give them some hope. The Otherway Centre, a haven for those released in Adelaide, provided names of detainees to those wanting to write to detainees.

The Adelaide Secondary School of English at Croydon accepted children into a 12-month transition program. Technical and Further Education (TAFE) accepted adults into English courses at minimal cost. Although many asylum seekers remain unemployed, some found jobs through employment agencies, through networking and through Australians who cared.

One of the initiatives of the Government of South Australia was to run an employment-assistance program in which refugees, aged between 15 and 24, studied English for 15 weeks. The program also helped prepare them for the workforce. It was a cooperative effort with the Australian Refugee Association providing case-management assistance and the English Language Services (ELS) of the Adelaide Institute of TAFE providing the English and workforce training courses.

People in rural areas of South Australia also responded, to support those who moved away from Adelaide. About 100 refugees found employment in the meatworks at Murray Bridge. Also, many found work in the winegrowing areas close to Adelaide and the fruit growing areas in the Riverland. Some families in rural areas also fostered unaccompanied minors.

Similar types of responses happened around Australia with many organisations involved in providing basic support services.

In Brisbane, a soccer team called Tiger 11 captured the public interest. It was made up entirely of asylum seekers, most of whom had fled Afghanistan. Club supporters, Camilla Cowley and Neil

Urquhart, had nurtured this team. In *ABC Report* (2 October 2001) Neil summed up what many found on coming into contact with refugees:

> I was like the rest of Australia, you know, oh, there's a group of boat people up there, you know, either turn them around, pull them out, sink them or whatever is the norm, what you are thinking of them, at that time. But after meeting them, I think that's where people have made their mistake. They don't know the individuals, they haven't seen them, haven't talked to them, haven't been involved with them. Once you do that I think you get a totally different idea of what real refugees are.

About 60 Afghanis found a new home in Dubbo, New South Wales, most of them working at Fletcher International Exports processing halal meat. The citizens of Dubbo showed a compassionate response in receiving the Afghans into the community and local volunteers even provided English language classes. It was a similar story with Young, another country town in NSW, which rallied behind a group of about 80 Afghani refugees. Employment group Mission Australia placed them in a Young abattoir. The managing director of Burrangong Meat Processors said that they were hardworking and should be given the right to stay in Australia. The townspeople offered free education and furniture.

In Victoria, a project known as the Asylum Seeker Project was established to provide support to asylum seekers through community and church groups. As well as helping in the provision of food, accommodation, medical aid and English language training, a special program called Linkup helped to establish contacts in the community. At Cobram, on the River Murray in Victoria, the townsfolk had responded well to an influx of Iraqi refugees, with 50 children bringing new life to the local school.

While these developments were taking place I received letters from some who were still in the Woomera detention centre and contacted some of those who had been released. I also received a letter from Sarwar in Pakistan.

Sarwar had tried so hard to come through the proper channels, as mentioned previously. He wrote to me enclosing a copy of the letter (22 January 2002) from the Australian High Commission Office in Islamabad in reply to his application for migration, sponsored by the Gawler Refugee Association in South Australia. After acknowledging receipt of Sarwar's application the visa officer stated:

> The current average processing time for a 202 visa at this post is 122 weeks, if all the requested documentation has been provided and there are no unexpected processing difficulties. Please be advised that this is just an average processing time.

In the middle of February, Majid wrote from the Woomera centre to say he was waiting to hear from the Federal Court. Sixty of his fellow Sabian Mandeans also had been rejected. Parvin had received her visa in January and had gone to Sydney. Farid had written a letter to the Minister of Immigration and was awaiting a response.

Habib and Rahim were released and were living with Haman in Adelaide. One of the detainees from Oscar had finally gained a bridging visa. With the bridging visa, though, there was no access to Medicare, welfare benefits and no opportunity to work. How was he expected to survive until his case officer made a decision?

Bahram was still in the Woomera detention centre. Salem, our Iraqi teacher, was released five months after being granted a temporary protection visa—a record length of time to wait following approval. Salem had been in detention for a total of 14 months. Later I learnt that Mohammed, an Iranian, at the Woomera centre had topped Salem by more than three months. Mohammed had spent five years in Korea for which he was unable to obtain police clearance from the Korean authorities because he had overstayed there. Despite being cleared by the Australian Security Intelligence Organisation (ASIO), Mohammed remained in the Woomera centre more than eight months after he was officially assessed as a genuine refugee.

I caught up with Aref soon after his release in a flat in one of the northern suburbs of Adelaide. There was nothing in the unit he shared with a fellow Afghani. He slept on a rug with two volumes of the Yellow Pages for a pillow. We went over to the Australian Refugee Association and arranged for some second-hand furniture and a bed to be sent over. Then with cooking facilities, towels, pillows and some household appliances he was smiling again. Later, Aref met a couple, John and Nina, who befriended him. They also assisted him in finding a temporary job as a seed-quality tester.

I met Amani, one of our other Afghani teachers, in a suburb nearby to Aref. He was learning to drive, had bought a mobile phone and found a job, along with other Afghanis, in the meat-works at Murray Bridge. Some of the Afghanis, he told me, had moved to the Riverland to pick fruit. Sadly, two had been killed in a motor-car accident.

Zahra and her husband, Haji, were living in Adelaide. They were desperate for work but their limited English was a barrier for most jobs. They didn't have a table or chairs but some members of a community service organisation, Soroptimist International of South Australia, came to the rescue and supplied these. Tayabba, one of the teenage girls so keen on typing, was there too. She was going to school and concentrating on learning English. Shaima was living nearby and had spoken at a meeting about the plight of asylum seekers. Hafizah had married and was living in Melbourne.

Parvin temporarily settled in Sydney after her release. While she had been in November compound five rooms, including the education centre, were burnt down. 'It was awful,' she said. 'There was nothing to do, no activity and no computer facilities.'

Everyone had known about her release before she had since

Dan, a security officer, had given a wink and a nod to her friends and they had shouted, 'Visa, Visa, Visa!'

Shahin and Samira had also settled into Adelaide life. Shahin continued to support Jeremy Moore and other lawyers of the Woomera lawyers group. Samira gave birth to a daughter in the Women's and Children's Hospital where I caught up with them. I just could not imagine how they would have fared if they had still been in the centre. If I ever meet their case officer I will congratulate him.

Even though Shahin was qualified as an interpreter he had applied for jobs in factories. He had been knocked back from over 20 positions in two months. He said that in some situations he had been on the verge of signing paperwork to start the job when he was asked about his visa status. As soon as he had mentioned TPV, the employers did not want to take him on because he was not seen as a potential long-term employee, worthy of training.

Of the other Iranians, Ali Reza also came to Adelaide and was looking for work as a primary teacher. Mehrzad, our other teacher, was in the centre waiting to hear from the Federal Court. Bijan, the relaxation teacher, was still there and wrote to me requesting some music cassettes.

Mouiad, who had assisted us in teaching, pined away in the detention centre along with his two brothers, Bahram and Roozbh, and his blind father, Bahman. As Sabian Mandeans, there seemed to be little hope—a heart-rending case of a curtain coming down on three fine young men, eager to work and have an opportunity in life.

Jamshid, our computer assistant, and his eight-month-pregnant wife, Ashraf, were ecstatic about being released in time for the birth of their daughter, Alisha.

Hassan, the chief negotiator for the Afghanis at the time of the hunger strike, was released on 14 March. I went to see him to discuss the events that had led up to the hunger strike in January. He spoke openly about the 'living hell' of Woomera, including a number of incidents during his eight-month stay, of violent behaviour and abusive language by the security officers. In one incident, Hassan said that a young Iranian asylum seeker had been stripped, bashed and held for two days in a police lock-up. In another incident, a woman had been handcuffed and confined in a cell in Woomera for two days without food and water.

Confining a person who had self-harmed had been a common practice, Hassan said. The ACM officer would replace the person's clothes with a gown. There had been no air-conditioner, fan or heater, no mattress or blanket, and the detainee was not allowed outside. When the detainees returned to the centre they had been traumatised by their cell experience.

Hassan had persuaded the management to stop the practice after the January hunger strike. From that time detainees had been taken to medical cells within the centre. The difficulty for many of these types of serious physical abuse cases was in obtaining evidence to substantiate the claims—unless, perhaps, the security officers were prepared to speak up. Up to that time, no-one— neither ACM, as care manager, nor DIMIA, as care provider—had been held accountable.

Aziz, our sports assistant, and his cousin, Amir, who did a first-rate job looking after the computer centre in the main compound, had to return to Iran—there was no hope for their cases.

Just before he left, Aziz wrote to me:

I would like to inform you that three weeks ago Amir went back to Iran. As soon as he arrived at home the Iranian Government arrested him. For the present I don't have any news about him. My application has also been refused in past days. I have got so tired from this detention. My family are also under pressure. As you know, I can't go back but for the reason that I have to help my family I am forced to return. In the event that my situation will be worse I trust in God. I wish you health and success.

Regards, Aziz.

Mehrzad also wrote:

I'm learning and I want to have a true faith. Every time that I learn one more thing about the life of Jesus Christ I can see a wider horizon. The light comes to show me the truth. Father Jim has blessed me for the baptism. I would like to say that I've changed my name to John.

I remember you almost every day and think about your respect and understanding toward me, and your patience in answering my questions. I feel I missed you during all this long time.

With best wishes to you, John.

Of the Iraqis, Zeyad, our computer teacher, found a job as a graphics designer with a foreign-language publications firm in Sydney. I caught up with Adnan in Brisbane; he had fallen in love with the city.

In Adelaide, Kazim found work in a seafood and poultry processing plant. Dr Amir told me he had been introduced to Kazim after his release. Kazim had been one of his students studying microbiology at the College of Veterinary Medicine, Baghdad University. He remembered Kazim as a quiet and keen student. On first seeing him in Adelaide Dr Amir recalled later:

I could still see the sadness and despair in his eyes. When I spoke about Woomera, Kazim became upset and cried out in anguish, 'Please, please, I don't want and don't like to hear anything about Woomera detention centre. The worst time of my life was there.' It seemed he was so distressed because of his detention, and I don't blame him.

Jan, who worked as a voluntary worker with the Australian Refugee Association, met all the Iraqis and invited them to share a Christmas lunch in her home. She has kept a motherly eye on them since. Among them were Thamer, who was released after eight months, Kazim, Amin and Mohammed.

Two of the unaccompanied minors, Anwar Ali and Mahmood, who had been so keen in class, were still in the detention centre after 16 months. On a brighter note, Imran was eventually released and I happened to meet him working as a welder for a manufacturing company, Blades Australia. The manager said he was an excellent worker as well as being able to communicate well in English. His keenness to study English during his prolonged stay in the detention centre had paid off.

Sapideh and Azita, the two young girls who waved me goodbye, were still there. It was definitely too long for them. They would be suffering a lot but how could you separate them from their parents? They both wrote letters, passing them on to Pam:

Hello, Mr Tom, I hope you be good. I miss you. I hope that cross I gave to Miss Pam you like. My letter is very short because I am afraid Miss Pam leave here. Bye bye. See you soon. Sapideh.

Mr Tom hello,
Excuse me that I have nothing that I send you. I don't think I can come to see you again very soon because we have [been] rejected. I miss you and I still remember your face. Never forget you. I would like that I had something to send you good teacher but if God we can get visa and we will see [you] very soon. Thank you for your picture.

Azita.

Jalil, our librarian, and Sima, his wife, and three children, must be at the end of their tether. Maryam, their daughter, wrote:

Dear teacher Tom
Very sorry, I can't send a letter earlier to you because camp is no good. The people are not eating. Some have sewed their lips and some are sleeping under the sun. I saw these things. I was very sad.

But now is better than before. We are going to move from the main compound. I don't know why.

After one month my Dad will go for a hearing in the Federal Court. I hope we will be accepted and please pray for us.

My wish is that one day soon my time here at Woomera will be finished and I'll fly to freedom like a bird from an open cage.

In hope of freedom

Maryam.

Cobra wrote to say she had been refused by the Refugee Review Tribunal and was awaiting the decision of the Federal court:

Dear Tom, I'm so sorry because Australia didn't like me, but I keep my energy and hope and seeing to future—to return to RRT and then if I can prove my situation and they believe I get visa, if not, I think I will do something wrong but I patient now. Sohrab every night pray for our freedom, I hope my God hears his voice and his prayer.

Cobra

On 28 March 2002, the start of the Easter weekend, more than 1000 protesters camped outside the centre. They pushed over the gates on Good Friday and stormed into the centre. About 50 detainees escaped. Most were soon arrested or gave themselves up. Two men reached Port Augusta before being caught by police. Jeremy Moore spoke for the lawyers representing the asylum seekers, saying that the violent nature of the protest was counterproductive and could even diminish the likelihood of asylum seekers being granted a visa. The chairman of the Refugee Council of Australia commented: 'The cost to the protesters of this incident was minimal—but the risk to prospective refugees could be considerable.'

Two of the 12 escapers who remained free after one week were Afghanis Anwar Ali, who had been so keen as a student, and Ahmed Fahim. They were taken to Melbourne where they spoke to a news reporter about their detention. Anwar Ali said:

When we were living in Woomera we feel like we're in hell. . . . Our life is not in danger but our mind is in danger. Every person became crazy in Woomera camp, even children, female, male, everyone. I think animals are better than us in Woomera . . . Nobody sees his future. I saw in my dreams I stay in Australia and I live freely. We love Australia, but I think the Government of Australia, they didn't love us.

(*The Age*, 9 April 2002)

About 300 detainees remained in the centre at the beginning of April. A new problem was emerging. Most of those remaining had little chance of being released. What would happen to the long-term detainees? How could families go back after spending more than a year away from their home? What would happen to them if they could not return home in safety or if there was no third country to accept them?

The effects of post-traumatic stress after fleeing persecution from their country of origin, aggravated by long-term detention, were becoming more and more apparent. Qadir, a Hazara and an unaccompanied minor resident of Woomera centre for more than a year, was sent to Adelaide's Glenside psychiatric hospital, suffering severe post-traumatic stress after fleeing from Afghanistan, where the Taliban had killed his parents. Qadir was diagnosed with depression, psychosis and suicidal tendencies.

One of the most distressing concerned Nadia, an Iranian with a disability and having to spend some months in the Royal Adelaide Hospital. Dr Amir was able to visit her regularly and give her some support. Nadia had lost all hope of being released and had tried to take her life. As a Sabian Mandean she had been persecuted in Iran. Because of the threat to her life she had decided to flee Iran with her nine-year-old daughter, Lida.

A South Australian report following an inspection by child protection officers after Easter raised more questions about the long-term effects on children. The report found that many young people were suffering severe mental problems. It also found that parents were not allowed to feed toddlers outside meal times and children did not have access to proper education, being offered a limited curriculum and restricted school hours.

Concerning the findings, the Social Justice Minister, Stephanie Key said:

> My assessment is that the conditions are not tolerable. The report I have received emphasises to me that this is not a place for children to be. It is shocking to think that some of the children who have been detained at Woomera for 12 months or more have never known any other environment. If some of these children are to be eventually integrated into normal Australian life, this is not a good start.

Jeremy Moore said it was heartening to see the Premier of South Australia, Mike Rann, taking the issue of conditions at Woomera on board. He told ABC Radio:

> It's wonderful to see them reclaiming Woomera as part of Australia and making sure, once again, we have decent standards and we don't allow children to be treated like this. One of the worst things about Woomera is that it's the largest amount of child abuse in the whole of the state and the perpetrator is the Commonwealth Government.
>
> (ABC Radio, 16 April 2002)

More than 70 lawyers, paralegals and social workers had now joined Jeremy Moore in providing their time and services for free to the detainees. Ray Hartigan was the manager and coordinator of this Woomera lawyers group. Assisting in the interpreting were those already released from the detention centre, including Dr Amir, Shahin and Hassan. The lawyers group had been visiting the Woomera centre for more than a year trying to extend an arm of friendship as well as give legal support. Elizabeth Boxall, Yasmine Ahmed and Tirana Hasan had forsaken practices with law firms to assist the asylum seekers. They had spoken to the Press often and passionately at public meetings, believing that the mandatory detention system was destructive and that we did not have to do it that way. It was great to see that such committed persons were helping give the asylum seekers a fair go. The true spirit of Australia was not lost.

Much of the advocacy work of the Woomera lawyers group was at the Federal Court level where no legal assistance was available. New legislation, restricting the Federal Court from reviewing Refugee Review Tribunal decisions, made the advocacy work even more difficult. The lawyers had also been trying to assist the long-term detainees, such as the Palestinians rejected as refugees. Some of them had asked to be returned home or sent to a third country but no country would accept them.

On a forum for refugee and asylum issues, 9 April 2002 at the University of South Australia, Christopher Pyne, Federal Government MP for Sturt, said that denying the conversion of a temporary protection visa to a permanent one at three years was a good thing because people in Indonesia who were planning to come to Australia would change their mind. Indeed, there was already evidence, according to Christopher Pyne, that this had happened. He had inadvertently let the cat out of the bag on a much bigger issue. The Government's main aim had always been to deter unauthorised people from coming to Australia irrespective of the human cost. The lengthy and flawed processing of applicants, the hardships endured in the detention centres, the crippling of people emotionally, the long-term detainees, the ones sent back, the difficulties faced by the TPVs, and even the riots and hunger strikes, all served a purpose—to send a message back to the countries of origin. Dr Amir confirmed from his own sources that the message was working—people in Iraq were taking notice and they would not come to Australia.

On 12 April 2002, the Immigration Minister, Philip Ruddock, advised that the Woomera centre would be scaled down but not closed in a shake-up of Australia's mainland detention centres.

What would happen to Woomera's 279 detainees? Some would be moved to the new Baxter centre at Port Augusta. The executive director of the Refugee Council of Australia, Margaret Piper, predicted that there would be further problems at Woomera and said that the centre should close down altogether. The council was concerned that it would still be used to house long-term detainees, 'the most stressed of all detainees'.

On 21 April 2002, the Show Mercy concert at Sydney Town Hall featured a number of stars including Noah Taylor, Jack Thompson and Max Gilles. The purpose of the concert was to raise awareness of asylum seekers and the conditions inside detention centres. About 2000 people gathered at the Town Hall concert calling for an end to mandatory detention. An eminent scientist, and the New South Wales Director of Public Prosecutions, Sir Gustav Nossel, addressed the gathering. South African Archbishop Desmond Tutu sent a video message urging Australians to show more compassion towards asylum seekers. Senator Bob Brown echoed Archbishop Tutu's request: 'The strength of a democracy is always in the compassion of its people.'

Then, psychologists Lyn Bender, Terry Zeecher and Glenda Koutroulis spoke out on *Lateline* about the deteriorating and distressful situation facing the long-term detainees at Woomera centre. It was no longer possible to detain and care for them. The daily occurrences of self-harm and attempted suicides in a 'hostile and isolated environment' were signs of 'desperation' and 'detainees had moved beyond the point of being in control of themselves'. (ABC *Lateline*, 22 April 2002)

On 4 May, Dr Anthony Burke, a lecturer in politics at the University of Adelaide, addressed over 200 people at a *Night for Humanity*, a fund-raising dinner for refugees. He stressed the importance of articulating a viable and workable new policy on asylum seekers and to repeat its benefits at every opportunity. 'Current policy on refugees,' he said, 'is being revealed as socially, morally, political and economically unsustainable.'

Dr Burke called for a workable balance in a policy shift between our sovereign rights and our human responsibilities. He focused on efforts to identify and prosecute people smugglers; to limit the detention period especially for children; to restore legal credibility to the assessment of claims for asylum (the main cause of anguish for asylum seekers); and to give permanent residency to people who have been granted refugee status. For those who cannot return home after not meeting the criteria of a refugee under the Convention, a special class of humanitarian visa for one or two years could help.

In a similar way, Chris Sidoti, national spokesperson for the Human Rights Council of Australia, had already outlined principles for a good refugee policy. He said, 'Present policy is reactive, piecemeal and ad hoc without any clear foundation in law or ethics, grounded in fear and government manipulation.' (*Refugee policy: is there a way out of this mess?* Racial Respect Seminar, Canberra, 21 February 2002)

On 9 May, Hassan, who had been released two months earlier, returned to the Woomera detention centre as an associate of the Woomera lawyers group. He discovered that a young woman had set fire to herself in a toilet cubicle after locking the door. She had also drunk detergent and tried to hang herself. The RRT had rejected her application. She had been so distressed that she had barely recognised her two children. Compounding the problem had been the confinement of her husband in a different compound. An Uzbek woman from Afghanistan had also been separated from her husband and six children, by first being put into a medical cell and then into the all-male Oscar compound. In another case, a man who had been in the centre for about 16 months had gone on a hunger strike. He too had been placed into Oscar compound, separating him from his wife and five children. One of his sons had requested to talk to his father but the ACM security officer had refused permission. The son had become so distraught he had tried to hang himself. Hassan had talked to a number of detainees at the centre, all with depressing stories to tell.

Hassan's visit to the centre prompted him to say:

At this time I can say there is no-one in the centre without a mental problem. I'm not in a place where I can criticise the Australian Government. On the other hand, I have to say something. I have an obligation to break my silence and to share my experience with the civilised nation of Australia.

I have a right to ask from the Australian nation to judge fairly between the Government and these innocent people, as I know Australia has not closed its door to people. But the regime is playing a kind of discriminatory court. When I was in Woomera as a detainee myself, I faced a kind of aggressive people running the centre. I was confused how a civilised nation could have such an aggressive and unacceptable people. And I couldn't compare the aggression inside with the community outside. I believed the things in the centre; that 85 per cent of people in Australia supported the Government's actions. But now that I'm released, I don't believe the Australia I am now experiencing is like that at all. I'm aware that Australia has a great humanitarian record and this nation didn't get it easily. They got it bit by bit. It's very unfair that they lose it so quickly.

I want to ask the Australian people, if you could put yourselves for half an hour in the place of those innocent people in detention— who have been detained for a long time without proper education for the children and without hope in the future, how would you feel? If you too were held in limbo in a non-healthy environment, where you witness self-harm every single day, where the children are crying, a place similar to hell, how would you react? If you had to suffer every day a place full of razor wire, a place where water cannons and tear gas spray directly into the face of children, a place hundreds of kilometres from anywhere—a testing place for missiles and unimaginably alien, what would you do?

(Racial Tolerance and Human Rights Conference,
The Otherway Centre, 16 May 2002)

On 17 May, I met the Immigration Detention Advisory Group (IDAG) to discuss ways of improving services for asylum seekers at the new Baxter Immigration Reception and Processing Centre at Port Augusta. Kevin Liston, Director of Australian Refugee Association, had initiated the meeting with IDAG. Air Marshall Ray Funnell (retired) welcomed and introduced me to Major General Warren Glenny, chairman of the Refugee Resettlement Advisory Council, Ellen Goodman, member of the Migration Review Tribunal, Dr Mohammed Taha Alsalami, a prominent leader in Sydney's Muslim community, and Gerry Hand, a former Minister for Immigration, Local Government and Ethnic Affairs (1990–1993).

We discussed the value of providing improved educational services and why only a third of the adults came to classes. I emphasised that the period awaiting the outcome of their claims could be spent valuably in a friendly environment with ready access by non-government organisations to assist in counselling and preparing them for settlement in Australia. There was general agreement about the value of this.

We went on to discuss the Australian detention culture that had evolved over the past three years. I suggested that this culture, involving hunger strikes, rioting, lip-sewing and self-harming, had become well ingrained in the detention centres and would continue to be a problem unless radical changes were made. New arrivals were often enthusiastic about coming to classes but would soon become depressed and despairing of their future as they absorbed negative elements of this culture.

Ray Funnell agreed and said that the ease of communication across the detention centres reinforced this.

Gerry Hand commented that he did not know the reason for the sad state of affairs of the detention systems in Australia, especially compared to other countries where there were much poorer conditions. From his overseas visits, asylum seekers in camps coped far better than in Australia; they were more resourceful and organised for learning and other activities.

I put it to him there were higher expectations for a country like Australia and they had been sold a story by the smugglers of a five-week processing period before gaining a visa. Coupled with this, the managing and processing of detainees at the Woomera centre had got off to a bad start from December 1999 when there had been virtually no progress in processing the claims of applicants until June 2000. The situation was not helped by the correctional attitude of the guards and the prison-like environment. Even for new recruits there was still only about half a day in six weeks of training given over to the importance of cultural aspects.

Warren Glenny commented that they were well aware of the value of this training and Gerry Hand said that treating asylum seekers humanely and in a culturally sensitive way should be an integral part of all training sessions.

Ray Funnell brought the half hour's discussion to a close and assured me of planning to overcome some of the constraints faced at the Woomera centre for the new Baxter centre. There would be no razor-wire fence. As an afterthought, he hoped that they would not burn down the much-improved teaching facilities.

As an afterthought too I wrote to Ray Funnell on 20 May 2002 to emphasise some of the points we had been discussing:

In addition to offering a more friendly type of environment for asylum seekers, which we discussed briefly, I believe the over-riding concern is still the processing of applicants' claims in a reasonable time. In conjunction with this is the need for applicants not to be held in limbo without communication on the progress of their cases; the need for independent legal representation; and the need to provide a category of visa, such as a humanitarian visa, that allows the asylum seeker into the community pending the outcome of their cases if not resolved within a specified time period, say, three months. The special visa would also take into account those people who wish to return to their country of origin or go to a third country but cannot because of political or other reasons.

If the processing aspects can be addressed then I believe we can offer valuable services in education, counselling and other activities, especially if we allow ready access of concerned people from outside organisations such as STTARS. If we are just improving the environment for asylum seekers in Baxter then I think we will ultimately face the same problems as we have had up to now.

Ray Funnell replied on 4 June 2002:

Thank you for your letter of 20 May 2002 and for the information and the impressions passed on to the IDAG during our recent meeting in Adelaide. I hope you and the other people with whom we met that day are aware of the importance that we as a group place on such meetings.

We continue to work at improving the lot of those being held in detention and we remain hopeful and, we trust, realistically hopeful of being able to bring about some changes in policy that will result in a much better system of processing asylum seekers.

Two weeks later, Jalil, our librarian, wrote from Woomera after the Federal Court had rejected his appeal:

Dear Mr Tom

Hello, how are you? We apply for Full Federal Court but I sure we haven't chance in the court. Two years pass and my kids not go to school.

We lose patience and soul and are sick and haven't hope. We saw too much riots in the camp and we are suffering. I don't know what to do. This condition is too hard for us. We are very tired.

Best wishes to you.

Jalil

In a similar tone, Bijan wrote:

Mr Tom, what are you doing now? Are you teaching English or not? Would you like to come here again? I don't think so because there is not anything new in here. Here is very boring. I don't think you stay here in this situation, now that it is a worse situation than anyone can imagine in here. Oh, Mr Tom, I got very tired, really—I'm suffering in here. Now everything is worse than before—there is nothing for amusement. Exactly, I don't know when and how we get out from this hell hole. It is so hard.

I hope for the best wishes for you.

Bijan

In response to a request by UN Human Rights Commissioner Mary Robinson, a UN Working Group of Arbitrary Detention examined conditions at the Woomera detention centre on 28 May 2002. Hassan, the Afghani delegate involved in the hunger-strike negotiations, informed *The Australian* that the rolls of razor wire separating the compounds and between the inner and outer fences had been removed just prior to the visit of the UN officials. The razor wire atop the perimeter fencing was still in place.

On the 13 June Elizabeth Boxall of the Woomera lawyers group and I spent an hour with Senator Jeannie Ferris going over a whole range of issues covering children and adults within the centre. These covered the deteriorating crisis with an impending hunger strike, the difficulties faced by members of the lawyers group in meeting with their clients, the plight of the 53 remaining children and the declining mental condition of all detainees. Senator Ferris promised to raise some of these issues in Federal Parliament.

Dr Amir informed me that Cobra had tried to take her own life and was in the Woomera hospital. The Federal Court had accepted her case and it would have gone back to the Refugee Review Tribunal but DIMIA had appealed against the decision and it had to go to the Full Federal Court instead. Cobra was one of the strongest women I had met in the centre and seemed prepared to ride out any storm with her determined optimism. But that hope had been crushed.

A new hunger strike began on 24 June. For the Afghanis, they had nothing to lose—it was going to be a do-or-die effort. They were joined by a number of Iranians and others but there were conflicting reports as to the number of adults and children taking part. ACM took away the mobile phones so there was no way of contacting them directly.

On 27 June 33 asylum seekers broke out of Woomera with the help of protesters. In the following 10 days, 23 were recaptured. Those still at large included the two boys Alamdar and Muntazer. Their father, Ali Bakhtiari, had been living in Sydney for two years having been granted a temporary protection visa—of no help for his wife and five children languishing in the centre for more than eighteen months and having their case rejected. Ali told the ABC that he had no idea if they were safe. I hoped they were, and not fighting for survival in the desert.

On 2 July the Human Rights and Equal Opportunity Commission (HREOC) asked Inese and me to give evidence at a public hearing, as part of a national inquiry into children in immigration detention. We explained to Dr Sev Osdowski, Human Rights Commissioner, and to the other representatives that the Woomera detention centre's education program was make-do because of the lack of classrooms, teachers and facilities—we even taught in the mess to try and compensate for this. It was ad hoc because of the lack of a suitable curriculum and because of the nature of the teaching environment. The lack of teachers and classrooms meant that there would be only a limited contact time and that we could not separate the children into appropriate teaching classes with regard to such factors as age, ability and background. There was no special program for children with disabilities; it was impossible to cater for students individually. On top of this, the centre's environmental atmosphere affected children's mental and emotional development. We improvised under the circumstances, but it was only ever going to be a token response.

A number of other people spoke on care and health issues. Dr Jon Jureidini, of the Department of Psychological Medicine at the Women's and Children's Hospital, said teachers were working in 'impossible' conditions and that 'it would be hard to think o f a worse environment for children'. A spokeswoman for the Association of Major Charitable Organisations, Beverly Hartigan, a social worker, said the detention environment was psychologically 'disturbing' for children, and that their drawings were evidence for its impact. 'Their drawings always depicted fences, barbed-wire, faces with tears running down their cheeks,' she said. The former operations manager, Allan Clifton, also attended the hearing; he gave evidence in private at the end of the hearing. He spoke to me briefly saying that he suffered a lot because of what had happened at Woomera; he had had a lot to tell from his side.

On day 13 of the hunger strike DIMIA said that there were 89 detainees on strike. Medical staff were monitoring the detainees and none had stitched their lips. On day 16, the hunger strike came to an end and in the evening TV channels showed pictures of the Immigration Minister, Philip Ruddock, smiling and proud of the new $40 million Baxter centre with state-of-the-art detention facilities for security and surveillance as well as the provision of health and education services. There was no razor wire; instead, a 4-metre-high electrified fence.

'

WOOMERA CLOSES

About three weeks after their escape Alamdar and his younger brother, Muntazer, walked into the British consulate in Melbourne to seek asylum in Britain. After being turned down the Federal police took them to Maribyrnong detention centre where they stayed overnight before they were flown on a chartered light aircraft back to Woomera detention centre. Their father, Ali Bakhtiari, was distraught and inconsolable.

Shortly after, the United Nations High Commissioner for Refugees representative in Australia, Michael Gabaudan, said that Australia's detention system was the most severe in the Western world, 'combining the three elements of being mandatory, indefinite and non-renewable.'

Justice Bhagwati, on behalf of the United Nations High Commissioner for Human Rights, Mrs Mary Robinson, made his report on human rights issues with regard to the treatment of asylum seekers in detention in Australia. He concluded from his observations at the Woomera Immigration Reception and Processing Centre (Woomera IRPC) that the detention of children, including unaccompanied minors, was a violation of their rights under the Convention on the Rights of the Child. The unduly long period of detention was a matter of serious concern and the human rights situation in Woomera IRPC was in many ways inhuman and degrading.

The Australasian College of Psychiatrists described the situation in detention centres as a mental health crisis. As evidence of this a number of detainees were released into the community for psychiatric care. An Iranian woman and her daughter lived under 24-hour guard at a suburban motel in Adelaide while the mother received treatment. A young Afghani, Qadir, was also under 24-hour detention, living with his migration agent on a farm in the Adelaide Hills. Qadir had initially been detained in a psychiatric hospital in Adelaide when the state public advocate intervened to prevent him being returned to Woomera.

In the expectation that entire families could live in the community, the Circle of Friends in Adelaide had developed a system that included a house and personal, financial and social support while awaiting the outcome of their applications.

At the start of 2003, 30 per cent of people (290 adults and 60 children) in immigration detention were in South Australia's Woomera and Baxter detention centres.

Majid, whose case was with the Federal Court, wrote from Baxter detention centre:

> About Baxter detention: Truly is worse than Woomera and very boring and limited. We cannot see outside even contact with other people that are in the other compounds.

As expected, though it was surprising it took so long, another outbreak of violence occurred. Three months after Baxter detention centre was opened, detainees lit fires on 28 and 29 December 2002 which caused more than $2 million damage. The headline blaze at Baxter triggered the lighting of other fires at Woomera, Port Hedland, Villawood and Christmas Island detention centres with an estimate of the damages bill of $8.5 million. The compounds Mike and November in Woomera detention centre were largely destroyed.

Following the fires, on 9 January 2003, Sadiq wrote to me:

> All families have been taken by force handcuffed, I can't explain how much tears they have had at that time, except some families who

live in Woomera Housing. I lost all my stuff, even my sketches in the fire night in Woomera, there is no telephone allowed for detainees even from public booth.

As judged by the comments of Australians to the media, the violence had further polarised the community.

Kevin Liston, director of the Australian Refugee Association, commented in *The Advertiser* (4 January 2003) following the violence that the causes of the detainees' actions had to be found in the frustration and desperation of people who saw no future for themselves. He said:

> The regularity and consistency of reports by former detainees, staff and visitors of harsh treatment of detainees in Woomera and Baxter creates a picture of a system that has lost its way.
>
> Detention has been promoted as a punitive measure to send a message to would-be asylum seekers who hoped to find a refuge in Australia. It has become repressive and soul-destroying. Cruelty and personal degradation are endemic in the system. It is evident that management and administration of the centres needs an overhaul.

Prime Minister John Howard reiterated, though, that the Government would not shift from its present policy of mandatory detention. As a result, a lack of moral courage in showing a humane response as well as a lack of imagination in coming up with alternatives characterised the Government's weak leadership.

On January 20, I spent two hours with Afghanis Sadiq and Ghulam at Adelaide airport. They had languished at the Woomera detention centre for two years and had applied to return to Afghanistan more than a year before. Finally, the necessary clearance to return home had come from the government of Afghanistan. Sadiq, who contributed to this book through his drawings, including that on the back cover, may have left but his artwork will remain in Australia as a testament to his artistry and indomitable spirit while in the detention centre. Both Sadiq and Ghulam seemed relieved, I thought, that they were finally getting out of Woomera.

On 12 March 2003 the Minister for Immigration, Philip Ruddock, announced that the Woomera detention centre would be closed in the following month.

By April 17 all the remaining detainees in the Woomera centre had been transferred to the Baxter detention centre.

Glossary and Abbreviations

ACM	Australasian Correctional Management
ASAS	Asylum Seekers Assistance Scheme
Asylum seekers	Asylum seekers who have come to Australia by boat are assessed against the Refugee Convention to see if they qualify as refugees. If they also meet Australia's health and character requirements, they are granted temporary protection visas.
Assyrian Christians	Assyrian Christians established their church in the first century. They say they have long been denied the right to practise their religion and preserve their culture. After the Gulf War, many Assyrian Christians living in northern Iraq were forced to flee from attacks on their territory by Iraqi forces.
Boat people	People who arrive unlawfully in Australia by boat.
Bridging visas	The Department of Immigration, Multicultural Affairs and Indigenous Affairs (DIMIA) may grant asylum seekers bridging visas, enabling them to remain lawfully in Australia until their protection visa applications have been processed.
UN Convention on the Rights of the Child	All children, regardless of their immigration status, are entitled to the full enjoyment of the rights outlined in the Convention. No child shall be deprived of his or her liberty unlawfully or arbitrarily. The arrest, detention

or imprisonment of a child shall be in conformity with the law and shall be used only as a measure of last resort and for the shortest appropriate period of time. Article 37 (B).

Country Information Service

The Country Information Service (CIS) collects detailed generic information from a wide range of sources, including the Department of Foreign Affairs and Trade, other governments, human rights organisations, international media and academics. It distributes the information to primary and review decision-makers.

Dari

Dialect of Persian (Farsi) spoken in Afghanistan

Detention

Australia detains all unauthorised arrivals in its territory or territorial waters until they are released on a bridging visa, granted entry to Australia or removed.

DIMA

Department of Immigration and Multicultural Affairs (1996–2001)

DIMIA

Department of Immigration, Multicultural and Indigenous Affairs (2001–). DIMIA administers the migration laws of Australia as it applies to the admission to Australia of both offshore and onshore non-citizens to Australia who claim refugee status.

Farsi

Farsi (or Persian) is the official language of Iran.

Hazaras

One of the ethnic groups living mostly as farmers in the drier mountainous regions of central Afghanistan. They speak Farsi and are mostly Shiite Muslims.

HREOC

The Human Rights and Equal Opportunity Commission is responsible for protecting and promoting human rights, including:
• promoting and understanding and acceptance of human rights in Australia;

- undertaking research to promote human rights;
- examining laws relating to human rights;
- advising the federal Attorney-General on laws and actions that are required to comply with our international human rights obligations.

IAAAS	Immigration Advice and Application Assistance Scheme
IDAG	Immigration Detention Advisory Group
Islam	The religion of the Muslims, based on the teachings of the prophet Mohammed as set down in the Koran, the fundamental principle being the absolute submission to a unique and personal God, Allah. Islam is divided into two main divisions, the Sunni and the Shiah, each having their own version of Islamic law and theology. Iran is the largest Shiah country in the world although the Sunnis form an overwhelming majority of all Muslims.
Kurds	The Kurds are an Indo-European people with their own history, language and culture. They live in a mountainous region, Kurdistan, stretching across Iran, Iraq, Turkey and Syria.
Mandatory detention	Immigration law requires that people who arrive in Australia without authority to enter must be detained until they are granted a visa or leave Australia.
Migration Act 1958	The *Migration Act* provides that for boat arrivals there will be: mandatory detention of asylum seekers (section 189); and holding in detention of asylum seekers until they are either deported or granted a temporary protection visa (section 196). In addition, there is no right for asylum seekers who arrive by boat to be advised of their right to legal advice (section 193).

Mujahideen	In Afghanistan, Islamic rebel tribesmen fighting a holy war.
Offshore applicants	Offshore applicants form part of the migration program in which applicants are selected in accordance with criteria contained in the *Migration Act 1958* and the Migration Regulations 1994.
Onshore applicants	Onshore applicants are granted a protection visa where Australia has protection obligations to them under the 1951 Convention Relating to the Status of Refugees and the 1967 Protocol Relating to the Status of Refugees.
Palestinian refugees	Persons and their descendants who lost both their homes and means of livelihood as a result of the 1948 Arab-Israeli conflict. About one-third of the estimated four million refugees live in camps in Jordan, Syria, Lebanon, the West Bank and Gaza.
Pushtuns	The largest ethnic group in Afghanistan. They are Muslims with a tradition of inter-tribal fighting to settle differences. A similar number of Pushtuns live in neighbouring Pakistan's Northwest Frontier Province.
Refugee Convention	Convention Relating to the Status of Refugees 1951. The Refugee Convention defines a refugee and establishes the principle of non-refoulement. A refugee is someone who, owing to well-founded fear of being persecuted for reasons of race, religion, nationality, membership of a particular social group or political opinion, is outside the country of his nationality and is unable, or owing to such fear, is unwilling to avail himself of the protection of that country; or who, not having a nationality and being outside the country of his former habitual residence as a result of such events, is unable, or owing to such fear, is unwilling, to return to it.

Article 1(A) (2) Refugee Convention. Non-refoulement is the principle that prohibits the forcible return of any person to a country where they risk facing persecution on return. Article 33(1), Refugee Convention.

RRT   Refugee Review Tribunal, established in 1993 to hear appeals against decisions by the Department of Immigration and Multicultural and Indigenous Affairs to reject applications for refugee status.

Sabian Mandeans   Sabian Mandeans, or Johannites, reside mostly in Iraq and Iran and have had a unique language, baptismal ritual and religion for more than 2000 years. They revere John the Baptist.

Shiite   A member of the Shiah sect, one of the two main divisions of Islam, which regards Ali, the son-in-law of Mohammed, as the legitimate successor and rejects the first three caliphs, together with the Sunnite books.

Sunni (or Sunnite)   A member of one of the two main religious divisions of Islam which regards the first four caliphs as the legitimate successors of Mohammed.

STTARS   Survivors of Torture and Trauma Assistance and Rehabilitation Services. The primary objectives of STTARS, a non-government organisation, are to:
- provide treatment and assistance to survivors of torture and trauma in South Australia;
- ensure that all survivors have access to mainstream services in the area of health needs;
- raise awareness among service providers of health, education, and other human services regarding the special needs of torture and trauma survivors.

(Other States in Australia have similar organisations)

Tajiks

Tajiks are one of the major ethnic groups in Afghanistan. They speak Dari and most are Sunni Muslims.

Taliban

The Taliban or the 'Students of Islamic Knowledge Movement' emerged as the dominant ruling force in Afghanistan from 1995. Their primary objective was the strict application of what they perceived was Islamic law.

TPV

Temporary Protection Visa, introduced in 1999. It grants a three-year stay in Australia to those who arrived in Australia unlawfully. The refugee must reapply for another protection visa after 30 months and will be ineligible in most cases for permanent protection. Temporary protection visa holders do not have the same rights as other asylum seekers recognised as refugees and granted permanent protection.

UDHR

United Nations Universal Declaration of Human Rights
- Everyone has the right to life, liberty and security of person. Article 3.
- No-one shall be subjected to arbitrary arrest, detention or exile. Article 9.
- Everyone has the right to seek and enjoy in other countries asylum from persecution. Article 14(1).

UNHCR

The United Nations High Commission for Refugees is the United Nations body responsible for overseeing international treatment of refugees.

WCC

Wackenhut Corrections Corporation

Woomera IRPC

Woomera Immigration Reception and Processing Centre

Bibliography

Crock, M. (ed) 1993, *Protection or Punishment: The Detention of Asylum Seekers in Australia*, Federation Press, Sydney.

Crock, M. and Saul, B. 2002, *Future Seekers: Refugees and the Law in Australia*, Federation Press, Sydney.

Human Rights and Equal Opportunity Commission 1998, *Those who've come across the seas: Detention of unauthorised arrivals*, Commonwealth of Australia.

McMaster, D. 2001, *Asylum Seekers: Australia's Response to Refugees*, Melbourne University Press, Melbourne.

Mares, P. 2001, *Borderline: Australia's Treatment of Refugees and Asylum Seekers*, UNSW Press, Sydney.

Wakefield Press is an independent publishing and
distribution company based in Adelaide, South Australia.
We love good stories and publish beautiful books.
To see our full range of titles, please visit our website at
www.wakefieldpress.com.au.

Wakefield Press thanks Fox Creek Wines
and Arts South Australia for their support.